TRAVELING THE

SILK ROAD

American Museum of Natural History

TRAVELING THE
SILK
ROAD

ANCIENT PATHWAY TO THE MODERN WORLD

MARK NORELL, DENISE PATRY LEIDY &
THE AMERICAN MUSEUM OF NATURAL HISTORY
with LAURA ROSS

Sterling Signature
NEW YORK

Sterling Signature
NEW YORK

An Imprint of Sterling Publishing
387 Park Avenue South
New York, NY 10016

Cover: Designed by Chin-Yee Lai
Interior: Designed by Alicia Freile, Tango Media PTY LTD

ISBN 978-1-4027-8137-7

Library of Congress Cataloging-in-Publication Data

Norell, Mark.
  Traveling the Silk Road : ancient pathway to the modern world / by Mark Norell and Denise
Patry Leidy with Laura Ross.
     p. cm.
  Includes bibliographical references and index.
  ISBN 978-1-4027-8137-7 (alk. paper)
1. Silk Road--History. 2. Silk Road--Description and travel. 3. Silk Road--History, Local. [1.
Trade routes--Asia--History.] I. Leidy, Denise Patry. II. Ross, Laura, 1956- III. Title.
  DS33.1.N67 2011
  950.1--dc22
                          2011006192

Distributed in Canada by Sterling Publishing
c/o Canadian Manda Group, 165 Dufferin Street

Toronto, Ontario, Canada M6K 3H6

Distributed in the United Kingdom by GMC Distribution Services

Castle Place, 166 High Street, Lewes, East Sussex, England BN7 1XU

Distributed in Australia by Capricorn Link (Australia) Pty. Ltd.
P.O. Box 704, Windsor, NSW 2756, Australia

For information about custom editions, special sales, and premium and corporate purchases,
please contact Sterling Special Sales at 800-805-5489 or specialsales@sterlingpublishing.com.
Manufactured in China

2 4 6 8 10 9 7 5 3 1

www.sterlingpublishing.com

Contents

A BRIEF HISTORY
OF THE
Silk Road

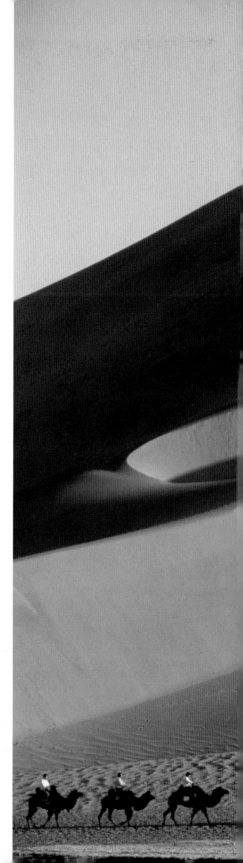

The Silk Road. It is hard to imagine a single phrase suffused with as much mystery and romance as those three simple, evocative words. What does the phrase conjure up in your mind? Exotic faraway lands, long-gone empires, and mighty conquerors? Punishing travel over blazing-hot, windswept dunes and unforgiving mountain terrain? Rich commerce in silks, gems, spices, and other goods—as well as ideas, religions, and ingenuity? The Silk Road embodies all of those things and more. By opening this book, you've taken the first step on a journey that will carry you across vast stretches of land and through thousands of years in time.

The Silk Road wasn't a road in the conventional sense (though it is sometimes described as the world's earliest highway); rather, it was a vast network of routes stretching all the way from China through central Asia to Europe, with links to routes leading north and south. It developed over many centuries and was traversed—in all directions—by hardy representatives from an array of disparate cultures. It was used to ferry a wide variety of goods, artifacts, innovations, and beliefs over the most challenging landscape in the world. The history of the Silk Road is inextricably bound to the stories of these cultures—their conflicts and alliances, their mutual influences and distinct characters, and their many gifts to one another and to the world.

At the peak of the Silk Road's use, during the Tang dynasty (618–907 CE), Asia boasted the most powerful empires in the world; merchants, messengers, religious pilgrims, and other intrepid souls traversed its network of routes every year. We will focus our attention on this fascinating time as we travel the length of the Silk Road from east to west—but before we immerse ourselves in this rich period, it is useful to understand a bit about the history of the region, and how "the world's earliest highway" came to be.

EAST MEETS WEST

No one really knows when, or how, the Silk Road began, but it covers a part of the world long traversed by nomads (of mixed ethnicity) who not only moved east and west but also north and south across much of Asia. Many nomadic confederations had ties to settled cultures such as the Achaemenid Persians and the Chinese, and goods from both these civilizations often appear in nomadic burial sites along the Silk Road.

The full development of the Silk Road can be linked to the existence of three great empires: the Han in China, the Kushans based in Afghanistan and northern India, and the Romans. The

A camel caravan crossing the Taklimakan Desert in Central Asia

Slaves building the Great Wall

Kushans exemplify the complex exchanges of peoples and goods along the Silk Road. Originally known as the Yuezhi, they were a nomadic group based in northwestern China who were forced out of their ancestral lands and moved west. Art made during their rule shows ties to Greek culture—introduced to Afghanistan and northern Pakistan with the conquest of Alexander the Great (356–322 BCE) in 330 BCE—and Roman as well as Indian and Chinese traditions. The Kushans, who were interested in many religions, fostered the practice of Buddhism throughout most of their vast realm. Many of the images of Buddhist deities from this region bear a striking resemblance to Greek and Roman mythological figures—evidence of powerful Greco-Roman influence.

Meanwhile, on the eastern side of what would become the Silk Road, an interest in the world at large was unfolding more slowly. A dark time known as the Warring States period (475–221 BCE) came to an end under the Qin dynasty (221–206 BCE), during which China was forcibly unified and its capital was established in Chang'an (now known as Xi'an, one of the places where we will spend considerable time as part of our Silk Road journey). It was during this period that the Great Wall of China was begun, its earliest sections built to hinder the incursion of the Xiongnu, relentless invaders from the north. The succeeding Han dynasty (206 BCE–220 CE) continued the wall's construction.

The earliest interest on the part of the Chinese in moving westward had little to do with cultural curiosity or even commerce. Rather, the Han leaders hoped to form an alliance against the Xiongnu with the Yuezhi (later the Kushan) people, who themselves had been driven westward. Toward that end, the emperor dispatched an exploratory group in 138 BCE, under the leadership of Zhang Qian. These intrepid explorers were captured and held hostage for ten years before they managed to escape and travel north. They finally encountered the Yuezhi/Kushans in northern India, though an alliance with them was never established. They didn't return to Chang'an until 125 BCE, and it is remarkable that the delegation ever made it back to the capital as they were captured yet again on their return trip. When they did finally return, they had much to share about the previously unknown territories to the west, not the least of which was news of a new, larger breed of horse that would certainly be useful to the Han armies.

Zhang Qian and his compatriots told stories that inspired the Han emperor to send new delegations westward, and eventually the missions traveled as far as Persia. Many credit Zhang Qian as the father of the Silk Road and date its beginnings as far back as the first century BCE. There is some evidence that small quantities of Eastern goods, including silk, did reach the West even before Zhang Qian's time, but the solitary travelers who carried these treasures must have been brave souls indeed.

This head of Buddha reflects Greek influence on Kushan art.

*Zhang Qian and his
fellow travelers*

The Wild East

It wasn't long before all manner of thieves and bandits got wind of the new trade routes through central Asia. Using their superior knowledge of the terrain to their advantage, they managed to plunder many a caravan. The travelers needed security forces—an expensive proposition. Forts and defensive walls were soon erected (including successive portions of the Great Wall), but even these weren't completely effective, and the Chinese lost control over portions of the road at various times.

During the period of the Han dynasty, many settlements arose within the Turfan basin—a topographical depression located inside several mountain ranges in the northeast region of modern-day China—to profit from the passage of travelers along the road. It was in these oases and villages that the locals absorbed the stories and culture of those passing through, and vice versa. The locals probably also acted as guides for the caravans, especially through the more dangerous sections of the route.

A Roman maenad dressed in silk

As time passed and one dynasty succeeded another, settlements came and went, the routes changed, and power over various regions changed hands. Towns thrived for a time and were then abandoned when the Chinese lost control of the region or their water supplies were depleted. When such settlements were deserted, they soon vanished under the driving desert sands, never to be resurrected. (Or at least not until intrepid archaeologists began to excavate the area centuries later.)

WHAT THE SILK ROAD WAS— AND WASN'T

The Silk Road's evocative name isn't nearly as old as the thing itself: it wasn't coined until 1877 by a German explorer and geographer named Baron Ferdinand von Richthofen (1833–1905), who first referred to it as the *Seidenstrasse*. Some of the subsequent interest in the area might even be attributed to the romance of the term, misleading though it may be.

Rarely did a single traveler or group of travelers undertake the entire journey from east to west or vice versa. Rather, goods tended to pass through a series of hands along the way, on a progression of different roads. A number of middlemen, notably the Parthians—a seminomadic confederacy that established an empire in Iran from 247 BCE–224 CE—collected fees and commissions as they ferried cargo along the divergent routes. Those involved in the process also exchanged news and ideas as they stopped for refuge and nourishment at the inns or *caravanserai*—so perhaps you could even call the Silk Road the first "information superhighway."

Early on, the few who did travel the full length of the Silk Road tended to be religious missionaries, though in von

An illustration of Marco Polo's caravan being guarded against an attack.

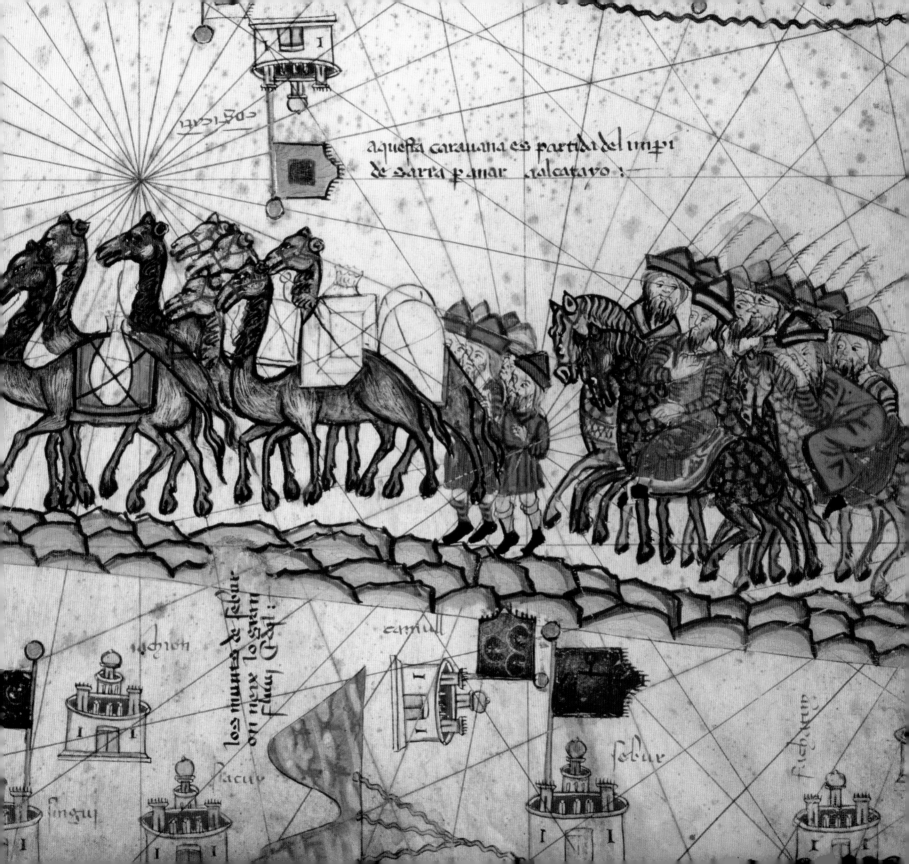

Richthofen's time, explorers, archaeologists, and historians took up the challenge. Today the term tends to refer to the vast area it traverses *and* its long cultural history.

The commodity that gives the Silk Road its name was certainly the thing that seemed most exotic and wonderful to those in the West. The Romans likely encountered silk as early as the first century BCE, via Parthians they took as prisoners. Correctly supposing that the relatively unsophisticated Parthians could not have created such an alluring thing, they learned that it came from a culture farther to the east, whom they came to refer to as Seres, the "Silk People." (Today, the process of traditional silk making is known as sericulture.) The luxurious fabric soon became the rage in Rome, and the Parthians—among others—seized the opportunity to act as agents for the desirable product.

But of course silk was by no means the only significant item traded along the route, which was very much a two-way street. Caravans traveled eastward to China carrying gold, ivory, gems, and glass; westward missions ferried furs, ceramics, jade, bronze, and lacquer. Since there is no evidence that Romans ever showed up in Xi'an or that Chinese merchants arrived in Rome, it is certain that many canny intermediaries profited handsomely from Silk Road commerce.

THE GEOGRAPHY OF THE SILK ROAD

If you are under the impression that traveling the Silk Road was strictly a sweltering, sandy affair, think again. These lengthy networks passed through all manner of terrains and climates, most being extremely harsh.

From Xi'an, conventionally considered the start of the road (though much of the silk that traveled along it was produced farther south and east), the route ran west through Lanzhou and along the Great Wall, through the Gansu corridor to Dunhuang—a flourishing oasis that became one of China's Buddhist centers during the early centuries CE and is a famous archaeological site today.

After passing through Dunhuang, the Silk Road split into northern and southern routes, both leading to Kashgar. The northern spur, which ran along the southern edge of the Tian Shan (an Asian mountain range) and the northern reaches of the brutal Taklimakan Desert, was less direct than the southern but was more popular, perhaps because it passed through such inviting oases as Hami and Turfan (which we'll visit later in our journey) before reaching Kashgar. The southern route passed through a different network of oases, including Cherkhlik, Niya, and

Left: A camel caravan in Afghanistan
Previous page: A caravanserai found in Uzbekistan

Khotan. There was also an alternate route that ran north of the Tian Shan mountains from Hami to Tashkent, Samarkand, and Bokhara.

Travelers worked hard to avoid crossing the brutal central desert—and I'm sure you can imagine why. From Kashgar, a number of avenues opened up to serve the purposes of a variety of travelers. Religious pilgrims could move through the Hindu Kush mountain range to the Buddhist centers of Gandhara and Taxila, while merchants could take a northerly route past the Pamirs mountain region to commerce centers such as Samarkand (where we will linger later). There was also a spur of the Silk Road running south of the Pamirs through Balkh and on to Merv in Turkmenistan. From there, various roads ran all the way to the Mediterranean, through Baghdad to Damascus or Constantinople (now Istanbul), or to the Black Sea city of Trebizond.

Between settlements and cities, travelers encountered the most trying terrain imaginable. It was some 2,000 miles (3,220 kilometers) across the area enclosed by the Tian Shan to the north, the Altun Shan and Kunlun Shan ranges to the south, and the Pamirs and Hindu Kush to the west. That aspect of the journey alone could take six months from east to west and a month or more from north to south. Temperatures (even in the oases) ranged from over 100 degrees Fahrenheit (38 degrees Celsius) in the summer to -40 degrees Fahrenheit (also -40 degrees Celsius) or lower in the winter, and constant winds kicked up choking dust clouds. Annual rainfall was only 8 inches (20 cm) or less. So where, you must wonder, did the water to irrigate the oases come from? The ingenious people of the area made use of the melted snow from surrounding mountains, pioneering sophisticated underground water systems, known as *karez* systems, that we will marvel at later.

The physical hardships of traveling the Silk Road, as chronicled by Marco Polo and many others over the centuries, surely added to its air of mystery and romance.

A sandstorm so large it could be seen from space

Deserts, Oases, and Encroaching Sands

The word *desert* conjures images of hostile foreboding environments—desiccated and scorching hot by day and freezing cold at night. But these images are not entirely correct. Deserts are areas of extreme topography, trivial seasonal precipitation, little animal life, and persistent wind. If you characterize them on the basis of aridity, the most extreme desert on the planet lies in central Antarctica, which hardly fits the picture of a burning landscape. Antipodean polar regions aside, the world's great deserts are belts that are nearly circum-global, found approximately between latitudes 30° north and 30° south. These include the Australian, Namib, Sahara, Mojave, Atacama, and Arabian Deserts, among others. In Asia proper, these arid areas compose one of the greatest desert systems in the world—extending nearly from coastal China to the Mediterranean.

Asian deserts are a heterogeneous lot comprised of features varying from stony plains bisected by glaciated mountain ranges to great sand seas. This belt can be parsed broadly and inexactly into subregions, like the

Caves found in the Gansu Corridor

Kuga Canyon on the northern edge of the Taklimakan Desert

Alashan, Lop Nor, and Ordos areas of the Gobi. North of the Himalaya, they can be grouped somewhat collectively from east to west into the Gobi and Taklimakan in central Asia, the Kizilkum and Karakum skirting the Aral and Caspian Seas, and the Syrian Desert lying farthest west. Each of these was and is a formidable obstacle to terrestrial travel. Combined they show how crafty, tough, and often lucky the caravaneers, soldiers, pilgrims, and adventurers had to be to survive. The traditional routes reflected the region's harshness, often taking the long way around, skirting the periphery. The camels, horses, and yaks lumbered along the flanks of mountains or through river valleys or ancient stream courses.

The Gobi is the northernmost Asian desert. It is a vast, rocky plain crossed and divided by the east–west Altai mountain belt. The Gobi, lying in modern China and Mongolia, is the least populated real estate in the world, outside of Antarctica. To bypass the Gobi a millennium ago, Silk Road travelers traversed the area along the banks of the Yellow River to the Gansu (or Hexi) Corridor, a narrow and relatively hospitable strip of land between the snow-covered Qilian Mountains to the south and the lower Beishan range to the north.

The most foreboding of the central Asian deserts is the Taklimakan. It is a sand sea, with mountainous drifting dunes distributed across a tremendous expanse. Standing on the edge of the Taklimakan, the desert appears as a vast ocean with undulating waves of dunes animated by changing light. The archaeologist Aurel Stein crossed the Taklimakan several times in the early 1900s. During these journeys, members of his expeditions suffered incredible ravages due to the

A caravan rests at an oasis.

Moving westward from the Taklimakan, the caravans moved into the Kizilkum and Karakum Deserts. Different from the eastern regions, these areas were better irrigated by rivers, springs, and the inland Caspian and Aral Seas. The major rivers are the Amu Dar'ya and Syr Dar'ya, variously called the Oxus and Jaxartes, emanating from the Pamir and Tian Shan (or "heavenly") mountain ranges. Although reduced to trickles by the thirsty needs of modern agriculture, these high glaciated peaks charged extensive aquifers until recently. Even though crossing these areas had its challenges, they were an easy part of the journey before or after the perilous crossing of what lay to the east.

The Silk Road journey sounds monumental, but in fact it was a local pursuit. No serious caravaneer would make the trip from Xi'an to the edges of the Mediterranean—that was the business of pilgrims and adventurers. When it came to trade, the experience was more like short-haul trucking. A caravan would cross a territory where the languages and customs were familiar and routes were imprinted into memory. A caravan would travel, offload the cargo, reload, and return by the same trail. But these treks were still formidable. Respite from the rigors of travel could only be found in caravanserai, often located at oases where constant water emerged from springs that supported habitation and agriculture. The deserts of Asia are peppered with many of these places, including today's cities of Dunhuang, Turfan, Bokhara, Merv (now called Mary), and Kashgar. Other ancient Silk Road cities, where the water supply eventually failed, were abandoned long ago and erased by the sands.

The harsh environment of the central Asian deserts is known for its extreme amount of aerosol dust. Strong winds, especially in the spring and summer, make for

harshness of the terrain. There was no constant source of water, so he crossed in winter—his water supply cached as blocks of ice lashed to his camels' backs. The extreme cold and hardships not only took the lives of several of Stein's camels, but he himself also gave up several toes to the harsh cold.

few clear days. Fog-like dust storms are so forceful and near steady that dust clouds often close airports in Beijing, cause health advisories in Korea, and color sunsets red on the west coast of North America. These storms can be so violent that the dust is injected into the jet stream, which can carry it for thousands of miles before it falls to the ground. Almost all of the dust found in cores drilled into Greenland's ice cap has its origins in the great Asian desert belt.

Historically, deserts subsumed many a thriving Silk Road city. Due to a variety of factors, such as increased agriculture, overgrazing, and climate change—a process which began several thousand years ago and is accelerating today—there is ongoing desertification occurring in Asia. Cities like Gaochang and Niya were abandoned and buried by desert sands nearly a millennium ago when their water supplies failed. At some of these sites, rows of fruit trees are found in the dunes—remnants of Silk Road orchards of apricots, peaches, and apples. Many of these localities also preserve Tang dynasty houses replete with furnishings. Owing to aridity, these are remarkably well preserved, providing a snapshot of life on the Silk Road. Although there are sporadic campaigns for tree planting and regulation of land use, the sands of the Gobi and Taklimakan continue to expand at an alarming rate, while the Caspian and Aral Seas are puddles compared to their historical extent.

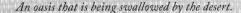
An oasis that is being swallowed by the desert.

MORE PRECIOUS THAN GOLD

As valuable as the goods that moved along the road were the beliefs that were carried from one culture to another. Buddhism moved from India to China along the northern trade route (most significantly during the fourth and fifth centuries CE, the period of the Northern Wei dynasty), and with it came Buddhist artwork and texts. As the locals adopted Buddhism, many monasteries, elaborately decorated cave-temples, and stupas (solid structures that hold relics) were built. The most passionate believers set off toward India, the source of their new faith.

The Buddhist grottoes constructed at the edges of the Taklimakan Desert during this period have yielded great riches to archaeologists interested in life along the Silk Road, because, in addition to their depictions of Buddhist deities and rituals, they feature scenes of daily life, local customs, and celebrations. The mingling of cultures depicted in the grottoes' murals is clear evidence of the influence of Silk Road traffic on the local way of life—and the mingling of blood itself is hinted at in the look of the figures (both human and divine), whose features are neither classically Chinese nor Indian but an amalgam of both.

Buddhism wasn't the only religion that wended its way along the Silk Road; Christianity found its way to China in that manner as well. In 432 CE, the Nestorian sect of Christianity (see page 71) was outlawed in Europe by the Romans, and its adherents were driven east to Iran. From that point, travelers carried the Nestorian faith along the road toward China, and by 638 CE (during the Tang dynasty, at the height of Silk Road commerce) the first Nestorian church rose in Xi'an. Though the sect no longer survives, it outlasted many enemies and thrived in the Far East well into the fourteenth century.

A cave temple found in Datong, Shanxi, China

The Great Stupa at
Sanchi in India

Manichaeism, an ancient Persian religion that has also passed into history, gathered adherents along the Silk Road as well. It was firmly established in China by the commencement of the Tang era and is represented in many Silk Road artistic masterpieces. For more on these religions see page 84.

PEACE AND PROSPERITY

The Tang dynasty was a time of relative stability and unity in China, after centuries of civil struggle and looming external threat. Peaceful times tend to promote the development and refinement of any civilization, and China was no exception: the capital of Xi'an developed into a thriving cosmopolitan city. By 742, its population had grown to some two million people, including at least 5,000 foreigners. Among its residents were Persians and Indians—who undoubtedly arrived there via the Silk Road—as well as Japanese, Koreans, and Malaysians from the south and east.

Our journey along the Silk Road will focus on this peak era, when commerce and culture thrived, and a modicum of civil accord freed the people of all of the Silk Road nations to turn their gaze outward toward one another, as well as inward, unleashing their own creative and spiritual natures. It was a time of scientific innovation and cultural fecundity.

THE FIVE DYNASTIES AND BEYOND

At the end of the Tang era, use of the Silk Road diminished considerably, as did the cultural flowering of the previous centuries. Attacks by neighboring states heated up again during the Five Dynasties period (907–960 CE), and it was not an easy proposition to get a caravan of goods over the Silk Road. Stability improved somewhat during the Northern Song (960–1126) and Southern Song (1127–1279) dynasties, but by then, the Silk Road had become less important for a variety of reasons, including the fragility of the goods being transported. Maritime trade was on the rise, and it made more sense for the safe transfer of delicate ceramics and glass objects. We will visit the "Sea Routes" as we round out our Silk Road journey.

From the seventh century on, the rise of Islam began to create tensions between cultures in the east and west, but it would be the schism between the Christian and Muslim worlds that put the final nail in the coffin of Silk Road trade. Beginning in the eleventh century, the Crusades carried the forces of Christianity close to central Asia, though the sultan Saladin's Muslim armies drove them back. Ultimately, during the Fourth Crusade (1202–1204), the Christians captured Constantinople—but it would be the Mongol hoards from the east who would split the Muslim world and take over the entirety of the region. In the 1200s, under the leadership of Genghis Khan (ca. 1162–1227), the Mongols enveloped the whole of central Asia from China all the way west to the Mediterranean: the entirety of the Silk Road. The Mongol Empire (1206–1368) survived Khan's death, and his descendant, Kublai Khan, would complete the conquest of China and establish the Yuan dynasty (1271–1368).

A battle scene from the Book of Kings *by the tenth century Persian poet Firdausi*

UNDER MONGOL RULE

As a pathway through the unified Mongol Empire, the Silk Road became an important means of communication again and trading resumed. Under Kublai Khan, who was surprisingly tolerant of religious diversity, a wide variety of people settled in China and traded along its routes. Daoism and Buddhism coexisted during the Yuan dynasty, as well as Roman Catholicism and Nestorianism. Jews and Muslims could be found in the major cities as well, though neither managed to establish a durable foothold.

It was around this time that European travelers began to arrive in China, the most famous being Marco Polo (ca. 1254–1324), the scion of a merchant family from Venice. Polo began traveling with his father at the tender age of seventeen—across Persia, along the Silk Road through Khotan, and finally to Kublai Khan's court. He returned west in 1295 and enlisted the help of a romance writer, whom he met while imprisoned for a year, to pen his *Travels of Marco Polo*. Not surprisingly, these tales, which were devised more as entertainment than as a work of history, are full of flourishes, embellishments, and out-and-out inaccuracies, but they have nevertheless remained valuable to this day as a broad and vivid portrait of the places Polo visited and the people and customs he encountered.

Silk Road trade under the Mongols was never as vigorous as during the Tang dynasty. Travel by sea burgeoned as the safer and easier alternative—and the cheaper one, as well, since it cut out the many middlemen involved in overland trade—although sea voyagers did face the perils of piracy and storms. Shipbuilding techniques improved, and new sea routes were developed through southern Asia. Ultimately, the choice between land and sea depended on the particular goods being moved as well as the level of political unrest at any given time.

Left: Genghis Khan

Kublai Khan in council with his courtiers and scribes

DEMISE OF THE ROAD

Successive Chinese dynasties (namely the Ming and Qing) became more isolationist, discouraging trade with the West and ultimately conquering the entire Taklimakan region and the territories of Tibet and Mongolia. By the 1700s, China was as large as it had been during the Han years—and quite autonomous—and traffic over the Silk Road all but ceased. It wasn't long before many more towns along its routes vanished beneath the desert sands, leaving only the most established oases as respite for stray travelers.

Interest in the Silk Road would not be rekindled until the end of the nineteenth century, when foreign countries began to think about empire building in the Far East. The first official British survey of India took place in 1863, and its earliest trade delegation arrived in Kashgar in 1890. By 1908, there was a British consulate there, and the struggle between the British and the Russians for dominion over the Far East (known as the Great Game) was afoot.

The Russians were the first to come upon the ruins of Turfan. The artifacts and manuscripts that they and the British carried back to the West ignited interest in the Far East, and soon the area was visited by geologists, archaeologists, cartographers, and other intrepid souls interested in the long history and diverse culture of the region.

The ruins of Gaochang, an oasis city on the northern rim of the Taklimakan Desert

THE ERA OF ARCHAEOLOGY

Sven Hedin, a Swedish cartographer, linguist, and explorer, first visited the area of the Silk Road in 1885, and it seems there was no barrier too great to impede his curiosity. He crossed the Pamirs to Kashgar and even led an expedition across the Taklimakan (though only he and two others survived the trip). Once he'd reported his findings to the world and exhibited what he found, the cork was out of the bottle: the archaeological race was on. The British, Germans, French, Americans, Russians, and Japanese sent expeditions, all attempting to unearth and claim as many artifacts as they could pack up and carry off.

The free-for-all ended in 1925, though, when the aggressive political actions of the British inspired a virulent antiforeign feeling throughout China. Chinese authorities began to block any delegations from the West and to insist that any archaeological finds remain in their country of origin. Nevertheless, many Silk Road treasures (including many that you will find depicted in this volume) found their way to the West. The largest collections are in the British Museum in London, and in Delhi and Berlin (though many of Berlin's treasures were lost during World War II).

This head of a male figure that was found in Karasahr, a Silk Road town in northwestern China, and is now part of the collection at the British Museum.

Silk Road Explorers

Until recently, most of what we knew about
the Silk Road came from the efforts of intrepid explorers
who traveled the central Asian Silk Road in the early
twentieth century. They have been called looters,
academics, spies, archeologists, treasure seekers,
and criminals. Depending on one's perspective, the
explorers were probably a little of each.

Their efforts were intricately connected to what
has been referred to as the "Great Game." It was sort
of a nineteenth- and early twentieth-century cold war
between Russian and British, and to a lesser extent
French and German, governments for influence in
central Asia. Later, even the Americans and Japanese
got involved. Dominion over the vast expanse of central
Asia was at stake, and from the British perspective,
protection of a land route to their precious colony of Raj
India and influence in China was at stake. To understand the area better, one of the primary objectives was
to make maps, erase "geographical blank spots," and
become familiar with local culture and power centers,
all while doing a little archeology and artifact collecting.
These efforts were contemporaneously chronicled in
a number of very popular books with titles like *Ruins
of Desert Cathay* (1912), *Trans-Himalaya* (1909), and
Riddles of the Gobi Desert (1933).

One of the earliest Silk Road explorers was the
Swede Sven Hedin (1865–1952), who began his explo-
rations in 1885. Hedin was not a trained archeologist,

Sven Hedin

yet he made important discoveries as a geographer, topographer, photographer, and explorer. During his numerous journeys across the Asian deserts, he found extensive evidence of lost cites (many in the Tarim basin) weathering out of the sands, abandoned because of conquest and regional climatic change. Hedin was a quixotic character—a devout royalist who later in life became embroiled with the German National Socialist Party.

Heavily influenced by Hedin's adventures was Aurel Stein (1862–1943), who became the most famous of the Silk Road explorers. Like Hedin, Stein was a great fan of the Chinese monk Xuanzang (602–664 CE, see page 75), and he was keen to explore the route of this ancient Buddhist sage. Ethnically a Hungarian Jew who was educated in Berlin, Stein had been fascinated by the Silk Road since childhood, and he came to the attention of the British Museum after his first self-financed expedition in 1900. The museum subsequently patronized Stein, who crossed the harrowing Taklimakan Desert several times, and his excavations of the cities of Niya, Karakhoto, and Dandan Oilik laid the groundwork for modern Silk Road studies.

Stein's greatest discovery was at the Dunhuang grottoes, also called the Mogao Caves, in 1907. These excavated caverns skirting the side of an ephemeral stream were places of worship and meditation for Buddhist monks. The oldest caves date to the fourth century. They are adorned with fantastic frescoes and statues of scenes that include everything from day-to-day life to surreal visions of Buddhist heaven and hell. By the last days of the crumbling Qing dynasty (1644–1912), the caves were in severe disrepair and were probably only saved from complete depredation by a Daoist monk named Wang Yuanlu (ca. 1849–1931).

Aurel Stein

When Stein visited the site, Abbot Wang informed him of a vast collection of manuscripts and documents that lay behind a secret wall that had been discovered during renovations. Inside contained the greatest repository of ancient Asian manuscripts ever recovered. The thousands of manuscripts, hidden for centuries, were written on everything from bamboo to paper to

A fresco depicting Uyghur princesses

News of the Dunhuang library traveled quickly, and soon the Frenchman Paul Pelliot (1878–1945) arrived at the grottoes. Pelliot, a talented sinologist, was able to select an important collection. His facility with Chinese (and thirteen other languages) allowed him to high-grade the collection, picking the best of the best. Like the others, he was also a man of many guises in that he traveled through central Asia under the auspices of Czar Nicholas II of Russia, who was contemplating an invasion of western China.

German interests were represented by Albert von Le Coq (1860–1930), an explorer and archeologist, known for the discovery of the Bezeklik caves at Gaochang, an ancient fifth- to ninth-century temple complex near Turfan. At Gaochang, von Le Coq discovered what he believed was a Manichaean library. Under the sands, von Le Coq found what many consider to be the greatest Silk Road masterpiece of them all: a series of life-size, carefully painted frescoes depicting holy men, pilgrims, and other Silk Road travelers. What is so unique about the paintings is their early date and that they depicted people of many faiths and nationalities. Von Le Coq removed several of the frescoes and transported them via Russia to the ethnological museum in Berlin, where they were immediately put on display.

Other nations were not to be left out of the frenzy. Japan sent Count Otani Kozui (1876–1948), a Buddhist monk. Ostensibly, Count Otani was in central Asia to explore the roots of his Buddhist heritage and collect important relics for his monastery and Japanese museums; however, he was viewed by the Russians, Americans, and British as an intelligence agent.

In the end, even the Americans became involved because many people did not want to miss out on the

parchment and were composed in a variety of languages including Chinese, Sanskrit, Sogdian, Tibetan, Turkic, and Uyghur. The trove included texts on Confucianism, Nestorian Christianity, business contracts, ledgers, astronomy, Daoism, and astrology, in addition to copious Buddhist works. All in all, Stein removed twenty-four cases of manuscripts and five more of precious relics. Unfortunately, one of Stein's talents was not sinology—the study of Chinese language and culture—and there are many duplicates in his collections, including several hundred copies of the *Diamond Sutra* alone! Today, these collections are housed in the British Museum in London and in the National Library in Delhi.

chance for their museums to develop important central Asian collections. Notable among these is Langdon Warner (1881–1955), curator at Harvard's Fogg Museum. Warner hurried to Dunhuang in 1924 on the heels of the others. He removed twenty-six of the best frescoes as well as several colored statues. During the frenzy the Chinese government, weak as it was, could not allow their artifacts to completely disappear and dispatched soldiers to Dunhuang to remove the remaining manuscripts.

From the time of discovery, the disposition of these treasures has been an inflammatory subject. Opinions about the legitimacy of the removal of Silk Road artifacts from China are all over the board. For instance, the copious volume of manuscripts removed from Dunhuang by the Chinese army dissipated to only a few by the time the caravans reached Beijing because so many were pilfered along the way. Of the artifacts that did make it to Beijing, many did not survive the depredations of war, rebellion, Islamic fundamentalism, and the Cultural Revolution. The objects also have even been used for political agendas as different groups have pointed to them as evidence of ancestral homelands in sovereignty claims.

Yet some of the objects taken abroad have not fared well either. Twenty-eight of von Le Coq's remarkable frescoes from Bezeklik were completely destroyed during Allied bombing raids on Berlin between 1943 and 1945, and Otani's treasures disappeared during World War II. Their whereabouts are still not known today. Even in the British Museum, only a small portion of Stein's remarkable collections is on public display. To the Chinese, the removal of these Silk Road treasures is still a painful wound, and travelers cannot visit the spectacular Mogao Caves (now a UNESCO World Heritage Site) or other Silk Road cities without being made acutely aware that many of the best objects were pilfered by foreigners.

Count Otani Kozui

THE SILK ROAD TODAY

Thanks to the writings of Hedin and others, interest in the Silk Road has never died—and today, many travel companies offer up the romantic notion of "walking in the steps of Marco Polo." The Chinese have taken up the archaeological mission where foreigners left off, and significant artifacts continue to come to light, preserved over the centuries by the severe climate and drifting sands.

Tourists visiting the Taklimakan can see the ruins of cities and grottoes, and a visit to the markets of Kashgar comes as close as possible to an experience of ancient Silk Road commerce. Tourism and travel in the western countries along the road ebbs and flows with the political climate—as it always did.

Travel along the Silk Road has clearly influenced civilizations all along its winding routes since before the Common Era, and though the politics of the countries through which it passes continue to evolve, and borders continue to be redrawn, it remains a significant crossroads of East and West—and our most direct avenue back to ancient times.

It's time to embark upon our own Silk Road journey—beginning in the venerable city of Xi'an—once the largest city in the world.

The Rawak Stupa in Xinjiang Province,
China, built ca. fourth century

Xi'an

CITY OF PEACE

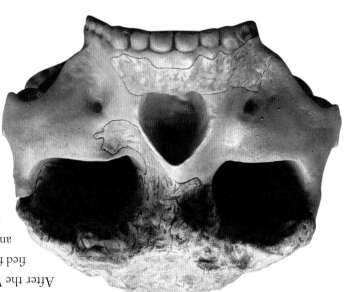

Skull of the Lantian man

A thermal spring in Xi'an

Our journey begins in the massive, cosmopolitan city of Xi'an, considered the easternmost point of the Silk Road. At the peak period of trade along the route, during the Tang dynasty (618–907 CE), this bustling metropolis was home to nearly a million people, with another million living just outside its imposing walls. Imperial buildings, temples, and markets lined its streets, and the city buzzed with activity night and day. Foreign merchants, ambassadors, scholars, and musicians flocked to this urban center, stocking the markets with exotic goods. The streets resonated with the sound of many languages.

HISTORY OF A GREAT CAPITAL

To wander through Xi'an today is to tread over layers of buried history. It is no wonder that the area is a mecca for archaeologists. Would you believe that one of their finds dates back 500,000 years? In 1963, a specimen determined to be that old, dubbed the Lantian man (a specimen of the wide-ranging hominid *homo erectus*), was discovered in Lantian County, just southeast of Xi'an. Evidence of a Neolithic Banpo village, a "mere" 6,500 years old, was discovered in 1954.

But the history of Xi'an as a cultural and political center really began in the eleventh century BCE with the founding of the Zhou dynasty (1045–256 BCE). The capital of Zhou comprised twin cities, located just southwest of today's Xi'an, known jointly as Fenghao.

After the Warring States period (475–221 BCE), China was unified for the first time under the Qin dynasty (221–206 BCE), and its capital was established at Xianyang, just northwest of contemporary Xi'an. China's first emperor, Qin Shi Huang (259–210 BCE), ordered the construction of a massive terracotta army as part of his burial monument—and it is one of the great wonders of the ancient world that we can visit today, thanks to its discovery in 1974 by some local farmers (read more on page 62).

A CITY BY ANY OTHER NAME

The name Xi'an is made up of two Chinese characters that can be translated literally as "Western Peace." But this important capital has had a variety of names over its three-thousand-year history. During the Zhou dynasty it was known as Fenghao. During the Han dynasty (206 BCE–220 CE), it was called Chang'an ("Perpetual Peace"). Though its name was changed to Daxing in 581, it soon became Chang'an again during the Tang dynasty, which was the golden age of the Silk Road.

During the Yuan dynasty (1271–1368), the city took on a succession of names: Fengyuan gave way to Anxi and then Jingzhao. It was first called Xi'an, the name by which it is known today, in 1369, during the Ming dynasty (1368–1644)—but that wasn't the end of the story. In 1930 it was renamed Xijing for a brief period until finally, in 1943, the name Xi'an was restored.

In Chinese, the name is sometimes abbreviated to either Hao (derived from its Zhou dynasty name) or Tang, a reference to the Tang dynasty. What has remained constant is Xi'an's importance as a great political, religious, and cultural center. When reading about the Silk Road, you are likely to see this city referred to as Chang'an, its name during the peak years of trade.

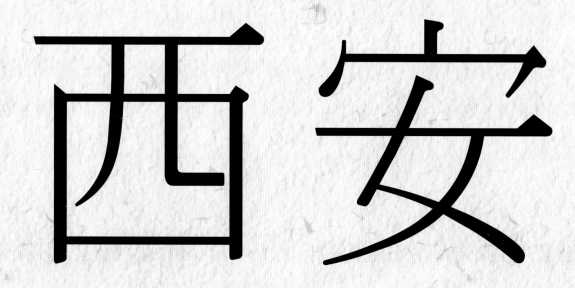

秦始皇

Emperor
Qin Shi Huang

Evolution and Revolution

In 202 BCE, Emperor Liu Bang of the Han dynasty established his capital in Xi'an, across the river from the ruin of the Qin capital, and soon a city wall was constructed to help ward off the onslaughts of competing warlords. After several hundred years of conflict, China was again united in 582, under the Sui dynasty (581–618 CE). At that time, the capital became the largest city in the world, consisting of three sections: the Xi'an Palace, the Imperial City, and the civilian section. In all, it covered 32.5 square miles (84 square kilometers), all enclosed by city walls.

By the end of the Tang dynasty the city was in ruins, and residents were forced to move elsewhere. A new wall, defining a much smaller city of 4.5 square miles (12 square kilometers) was constructed in the 1300s during the Ming dynasty, and that's the wall—and the city—that remain today.

In our time, Xi'an has continued to be a center of political action and change. In 1911, during the revolution in which China's last dynasty was overthrown, the Manchus living in the northeastern area of the city were massacred. In 1936, during the Chinese Civil War, the city was the site of what is referred to as the Xi'an Incident, bringing the Kuomintang and Communist parties of China to a truce so that they could form a united front against the invading Japanese.

Xi'an Today

Today, the population of of Xi'an has today swelled to more than eight million. In addition to hosting throngs of archaeologists from all over the world, it is a thriving tourist destination with a diverse and growing local economy.

Contemporary Xi'an is a place of manufacturing and commerce, featuring a wide variety of modern industries. Because it is located at the center of an area rich in natural resources such as coal and oil, Xi'an produces much of China's energy. As a result, the city is covered with a layer of smog during most seasons. In addition to its hard-working factories, it is the site of several major universities, attended by students from throughout China and the far east.

Sericulture thrives in Xi'an just as it did in Silk Road days, thanks to a number of active silk factories that keep the traditional art and craft alive. (Some of these are open to tourists.) It is also famous for its tender and artfully folded dumplings that can be ordered with a wide variety of fillings. These treats can be found at the outdoor markets that dot the city.

Besides the tomb of Emperor Qin and the terracotta army, other significant sites to visit in Xi'an can be found in the old part of town, inside the city walls. They include the Buddhist Big and Little Wild Goose Pagodas, constructed around the turn of the eighth century, and the Bell and Drum Towers, huge structures built during the Ming Dynasty to house the city's official bell and drum. Nearby is the historic Muslim Quarter.

Left: Little Wild Goose Pagoda

Previous page: The city wall around Xi'an

Soldiers of Clay

One of the first things that an ancient emperor, general, or other important figure did upon assuming power was plan and construct his own tomb. As China's first emperor, Qin Shi Huang was no different—and he intended his burial monument to rival any that had come before or would follow.

The work would take thirty-nine years to complete and involve some 700,000 workers; everything about it was intended to be grandiose. When complete, it covered 22 square miles (56.25 square kilometers). According to written accounts, among the many wonders the tomb featured were pearls embedded in its ceiling to represent the stars and one hundred rivers and lakes fashioned from silvery mercury in the floor. The highlight of the enterprise was a phalanx of 8,000 life-size figures that comprised an army replete with warriors, generals, officials, and chariots. These statues were arranged in four pits surrounding Qin Shi Huang's tomb and were meant to protect the ruler and his next empire in the afterlife.

You could say that the terracotta army, inanimate as it was, saved many lives. Based on a tradition known as *Xun*—quite barbaric to our contemporary sensibilities—it was common practice for living people, sometimes numbering in the hundreds, to be interred along with members of the Qin ruling class and provide protection and other services in the afterlife. (For example, when Duke Mu of Qin died in 621 BCE, 177 slaves and followers were buried with him.) The clay soldiers

A close-up of the life-size warriors

Row after row of warriors have been uncovered.

pits about 23 feet (7 meters) deep. The first pit, 754 feet (230 meters) long, contains figures that comprise the main army, spread out along eleven corridors paved with bricks. The second pit holds cavalry and infantry units and chariots, while the third pit is thought to have represented a command post, housing high-ranking officers. The fourth and final pit is empty; it is believed to have been left unfinished by its builders.

Representative figures from the terracotta army, along with other artifacts, have traveled to museums all over the world, attracting unprecedented crowds, but the best way to view these astonishing relics is to visit the original site, which is still being excavated.

were certainly a more humane solution—though, in customary fashion, Qin Shi Huang did have the artisans who designed and built his tomb put to death so they could not reveal its secrets. Those secrets still lie buried with the emperor: although the terracotta army has been uncovered, the tomb itself has yet to be opened.

Great artistry went into fashioning the clay soldiers. The lifelike figures were cast in a variety of molds. The pieces then would be fitted together to create thousands of seemingly unique soldiers. The array of parts used to create them allowed their heights, their ranks, and even the draping and fit of their uniforms to appear distinctive.

In 1974, during the Cultural Revolution, local farmers digging a well first stumbled upon the figures, captivating the attention of archaeologists, who immediately set about excavating the site. They unearthed four

Warriors in battle formation

SECRETS OF SILK

Xi'an has always figured prominently in the creation of the vibrant fabric that gave the Silk Road its name. From Westerners' first glimpse of this luxurious textile, the world has been captivated by the ancient and mysterious art of silk making—and today's methods are not all that different from those pioneered by artisans thousands of years ago. It all begins with the cultivation of silkworms.

It's hard to believe that the source of the cloth we use to make expensive scarves, dresses, ties, and gowns is a little white caterpillar—but that's the case. For thousands of years, silk farmers, first in China and then around the world, have raised silkworms and harvested their silk.

The Life of a Silkworm

Both wild and domesticated silk moths produce silk, but the best-quality filaments come from the domesticated silkworm moth, *Bombyx mori.* Descended from a species native to China, these silk moths are helpless: they are blind, flightless, and can only live in captivity.

Adult silk moths mate, the female soon lays about five hundred tiny eggs—and then she dies. After about ten to twelve days, a minuscule caterpillar hatches out of each egg. The little caterpillars grow quickly as they feed on mulberry leaves, multiplying their weight 10,000 times in only one month. As a result, they continually "outgrow" their whitish gray skin and shed it three or four times before they reach full size.

The mature caterpillar soon spins a silk cocoon around itself and, once safely inside, begins its transformation into a pupa. If left to its own devices, the pupa emerges from its cocoon as a moth and begins the life cycle all over again. In silk cultivation, however, the farmers interrupt the natural cycle by collecting the cocoons before the moths are ready to hatch. They unwind the cocoons into silk threads, which are then woven into cloth.

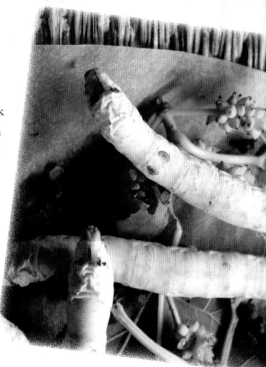

Silkworm moth caterpillars

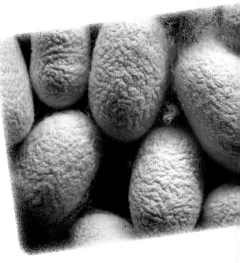

Silkworm moth cocoons

SILK SPINNERS

Silkworms aren't the only creatures that spin silk. Spiders also can, along with certain kinds of bees, wasps, and ants. But silkworms are the only ones that produce threads we find worthwhile to weave into cloth.

Secret History

The secrets of silk, carefully guarded for centuries, brought wealth and prestige to a succession of Chinese empires. Early silk farmers, often helped by their children, would carefully weigh and sort cocoons by their size and quality. The cocoons were then dunked in boiling water to loosen the filaments, several of which were pulled together to form a thread, which was then wound onto a reel. Workers would then stretch bundles of the silk thread—called skeins—onto a wooden frame and rewind them onto smaller reels.

At that point, it was time to make the fabric. The earliest silk weavers spent weeks or even months working by hand to make enough fabric for a single garment. Luckily, by the time of

Here silkworm cocoons are being placed in baskets.

This painting from the early thirteenth century depicts the process of silk making in China.

In this panel, women are preparing the silkworm eggs so the caterpillars can hatch.

LOOM LESSONS

Foot pedals—called treadles—raise individual warp threads, allowing weavers to pass the horizontal weft threads in between.

Weavers string long warp threads along the length of the loom.

By pressing different treadles, weavers raise different warp threads and then pass the weft thread back through.

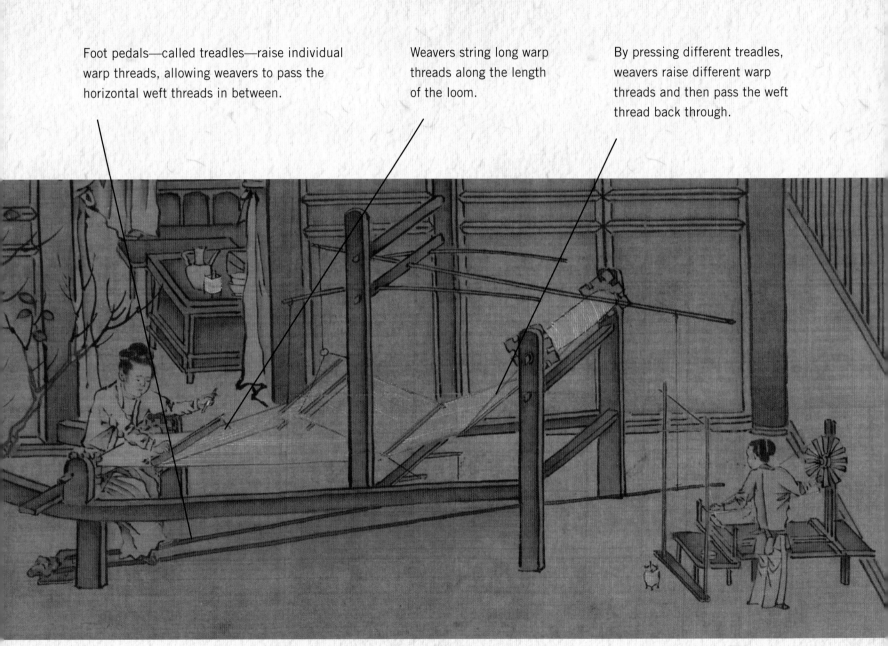

Finished cloth consists of interlaced warp and weft threads. Looms allow weavers to change the interlacement easily, thereby creating complicated patterns.

In this panel, women are preparing the silkworm eggs so the caterpillars can hatch.

Here the cocoons are being sorted, spun into thread, and weaved into cloth.

the Silk Road, when demand for silk was rampant, looms made it possible to work much faster and to create a wide array of intricately patterned fabrics, from chiffons to satins. Different-colored threads, complex dying techniques, and designs embroidered into the woven cloth further enhanced the exquisite Chinese silks of the period.

When China was the only source of silk cloth in the world—because only they knew how to make it—the fabric was so desired that foreign weavers would trade for Chinese silks, unwind the threads, then reweave them into new garments. China recognized the value of its secret and carefully guarded the process, threatening anyone sharing it with death. But no secrets last forever. Eventually the art of silk making spread throughout the Western world.

LOOM LESSONS

Foot pedals—called treadles—raise individual warp threads, allowing weavers to pass the horizontal weft threads in between.

Weavers string long warp threads along the length of the loom.

By pressing different treadles, weavers raise different warp threads and then pass the weft thread back through.

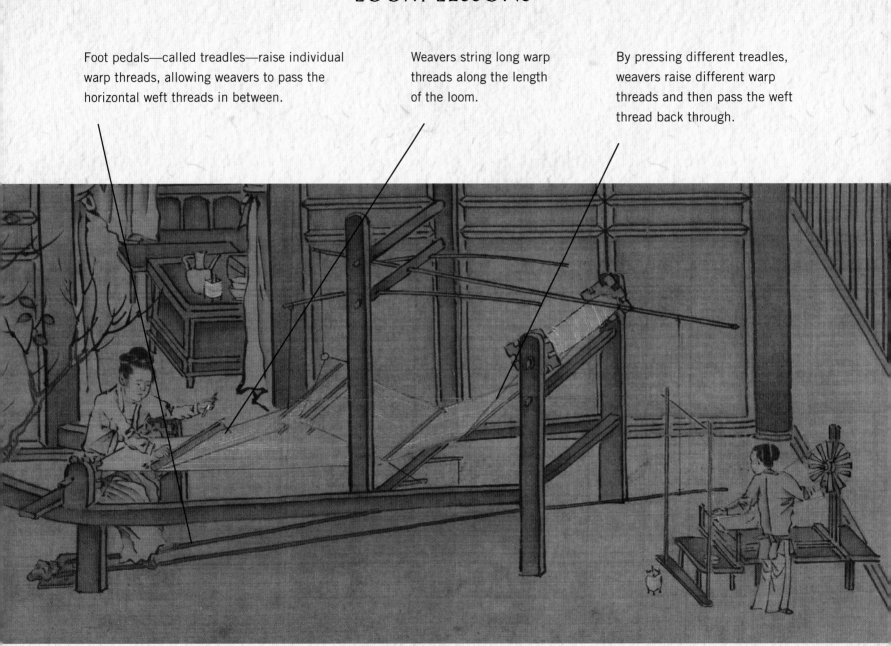

Finished cloth consists of interlaced warp and weft threads. Looms allow weavers to change the interlacement easily, thereby creating complicated patterns.

Dream Fabric

Once you've held a bolt of silk, it's easy to imagine why the first silk cloth must have seemed magical. It is strong and sturdy, but also soft and luxurious. Silk clothing is cool in the summer and warm in the winter. The earliest silks were so rare and costly that only the royal family could wear them, but over time, as more farmers began to raise silkworms and weave cloth, silk clothing became more accessible.

The intricate silk patterns shown on these pages are just a few of the many that the Tang silk makers used to decorate their fine fabrics, utilizing a wide variety of sophisticated techniques. Silk truly is the fabric of dreams.

Court ladies preparing freshly woven silk

Silk Throughout History

With time and patience the mulberry leaf becomes a silk gown.

—Chinese proverb

I can see clothes of silk, if materials that do not hide the body, nor even one's decency, can be called clothes.

—Seneca the Younger, *Declamations, Vol. 1*

Silk is an amazing substance. It is a light fabric, yet it is strong, diaphanous, and clingy. It is capable of keeping a body warm and cool while looking great at the same time. It is no wonder that silk remains a precious commodity arguably five millennia since it was first harvested. The first question that comes to mind: Who came up with the brilliant idea that the silk strands spun by the caterpillar of the silk moth could be separated and woven into luxurious cloth?

There is a Chinese legend that Lei Zu, the wife of the Yellow Emperor, discovered silk almost five thousand years ago. The story goes that she was enjoying tea in the shade of a mulberry tree when a cocoon fell into her steaming cup. The cocoon began to unravel slowly, producing a silken thread. Amazed by its fine and unusual consistency, luminosity, and strength, she gathered more cocoons and freed the threads—enough to intertwine and produce threads that could be woven together.

Undoubtedly this is apocryphal. How sericulture—the breeding of silkworms for their silk—was initiated, or even when and where, is a mystery. What is known from archeology is that the earliest incidence of a silk culture that can be definitively dated is from between 4000 and 3000 BCE in central China. This is based on the presence of silk cocoons associated with remains from

Silk thread

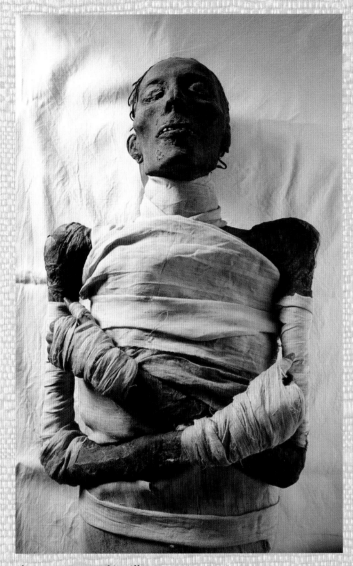

A mummy wrapped in silk

of actual silk fabric are shreds from Zhejiang in southern coastal China that are almost three thousand years old.

By the second century BCE silk was in mass production, and China had established organized trade with the West. Chinese leadership, knowing what a precious commodity they had, made it a capital crime to spill the secret of sericulture beyond the imperial domain. Nevertheless, by the middle of the sixth century silk was being produced in such far-off lands as Anatolia, Sicily, and the Nile Delta.

The earliest record in the West comes from silken threads found with three-thousand-year-old Egyptian mummies. Yet detailing the first mention of silk in European, western Asian, or other Mediterranean texts is difficult. Suffice it to say that silk was known by the Roman Empire to originate in the land of the Seres—the root of the Western word for sericulture—and, as suggested above, organized trade via the Silk Road began in this period. Early on, because the silk secret was still undiscovered, the Romans had no idea what produced it. Contemporary word on the street was that, like flax, it was the product of a plant.

Silk production finally reached the West through Byzantium in the sixth century. One legend has it that silk cocoons were smuggled out of China in the hollowed-out staffs of Byzantine monks—difficult to believe since the journey across the hardest parts of middle Asia would have taken much longer than the ten to twelve days it takes for a silk worm to metamorphose after the cocoon is formed. Another legend holds that the king of a country called Khotan—today, a city in western China—married a Tang princess. When she crossed the border, guards searched her caravan but not her headdress where she had hidden silkworm eggs and mulberry seeds.

the Yangshao culture that existed along China's Yellow River. But since even today silkworms are used as food in China, it cannot be unquestionably claimed that these cocoons are evidence of sericulture. The first remnants

The natural history of silk is interesting in its simplicity. The silk moth is a unique insect because it cannot survive outside of human husbandry. Left alone to the wilds, even in delicate temperate climates, the moths and their caterpillars will die if exposed to the natural elements. They are also extremely susceptible to changes in temperature and humidity. People who raise silkworms traditionally don't like visitors and don't cook heavily scented foods or even smoke cigarettes in their homes. The doors of their houses are usually posted with paper signs announcing when the worms are in a fragile stage.

After a silkworm spins its cocoon over the course of two to three days, the cocoons are harvested. Only a few moths are allowed to emerge and reproduce to provide the next generation. The individual cocoons are processed by immersion in scalding water, killing the metamorphosing moth and relaxing the single silk thread that comprises the entire cocoon so it can be drawn from the boiling water.

Silk itself is a complex protein, which when secreted is triangular in cross section. This structure causes reflected light to be broken up, giving silk its unique shimmering property. Each cocoon can provide about a mile-long silk filament; however, it is so fine that it takes up to five hundred cocoons to make a six-ounce silk robe. Although other kinds of "silk" from different species of moths (and even spiders) have been used to make fabrics, practically all silk fabric ever produced comes from this single domestic species.

Historically, silk has had all sorts of different uses. In antiquity, padded silk was used for battle armor as protection against arrows. Silk has been used for decorative items such as rugs, wall coverings, draperies, upholstery, and canvases for painting. It has even been used as currency. But its most obvious application has been for garments. Its sheerness has graced many a fine leg, and its translucent, body-hugging nature caused scandal in antiquity, as it occasionally does today on fashion runways around the world. There are even numerous contemporary statements that the Qur'an prohibits Muslim men from wearing the fabric.

Even after all these centuries, silk is still economically important. Obviously most of the silk that is produced today is used in the apparel industry, which employs millions of people across the planet. However, industrial and medical applications exist. In most cases silk is hypoallergenic, and this combined with its strength makes silk thread ideal for sutures and other medical applications. Until the advent of synthetic fibers, which began roughly after World War II, the demand for industrial silk was high as it was used for everything from parachutes to the lining of bicycle tires. Although industrial silk use has quelled, the textile industry is burgeoning, and more silk is being produced than ever. Production largely remains close to its presumed historical locale, as well more than half of today's silk is created in China, with India a distant second.

In this painting from 550 CE, the princess's attendant points out her secret.

BORROWED FROM ABROAD

Chinese silks were prized throughout Asia for their vibrant colors and superior patterns—yet those patterns often reflected the influence of other cultures. For instance, pearl roundels—circles of small dots enclosing another image—are common in Persian artworks of the period, including textiles, ceramics, and metalwork. Roundels appear frequently in Tang silks, reinterpreted as a Chinese form, as seen in this example from ca. 800. This is what we mean when we talk about the cultural influence of Silk Road travel. As people moved along the road, cultures, ideas, and art forms mixed and mingled, leading to hybrid forms that were often more than the sum of their various parts.

FOREIGN INFLUENCES

Xi'an in the early centuries of the Common Era was unlike any other city of its time. Foreigners from far and wide flocked there, bringing strange goods and exotic tastes. It was there, as much as anywhere along the route, that the social, cultural, and religious exchanges facilitated by Silk Road trade could be felt.

Many of Xi'an's more than one million residents were from outside China, and some had traveled hundreds or thousands of miles by foot, boat, horse, and camel to get there. Nearly every aspect of life in Xi'an—from music to cuisine to decoration—was influenced by foreign cultures and styles. The rise of Buddhism in China also encouraged an interest in the exotic, as Chinese monks made pilgrimmages to India and returned laden with religious texts as well as goods collected along the way.

These three statues from China show foreigners from different lands.

Silver Bowl

Precious metal objects reached China from Persia (modern Iran) by the Silk Road—and Chinese artists quickly adopted the style. This silver bowl from ca. 700 is Chinese in shape and is decorated with animals in Chinese styles. The floral imagery, however, is inspired by Persian motifs and the repeating lotus pedal shapes are common in Buddhist imagery.

Rhyton

Rhytons—cups made in the shape of horns—were common in West Asia and the Mediterranean but became popular in China as travelers brought them east along the Silk Road. This vessel was made around 750 in East Asia but shows a foreign figure drinking.

Wine Peddler

Wine made from rice or barley was popular in China long before the Tang dynasty. But as the Tang empire expanded west into regions where grapes grew, grape wine burst onto the scene. This figure, made in China more than 1,000 years ago, depicts a wine peddler who is not Chinese, but is likely Central Asian.

RELIGIONS OF THE ROAD

Silks, gemstones, and spices were not the only things traded on the Silk Road. Missionaries and merchants carried their own religions over its treachorous pathways—and encountered new faiths at the same time. And it wasn't just person-to-person encounters that disseminated religious beliefs. Travelers who wanted to practice their faiths during their long journeys built shrines and temples along the way, which were in turn visited by others. In this way, locals and foreign travelers were introduced to new belief systems. In some instances, missionaries established stationary religious communities for the traveling faithful and recruited converts in new lands.

Portable Shrines

Buddhist monks and devotees often carried small shrines as they traveled the Silk Road. Made of stone, wood, and at times more precious materials such as ivory, these shrines show scenes from the lifetime of the historical Buddha (now revered as Shakyamuni) as well as more complicated images based on the rapid development of Buddhist thought and imagery that occurred after the fourth century CE. A squatting, bearded figure carrying a large basket on his back decorates the exterior of one side of the portable stone shrine shown here. It was made in the ancient region of Gandhara (roughly present-day Pakistan) around the fifth or sixth century. It is not possible to determine the ethnicity of this figure, who also supports a child (now headless) on his back. His tall boots are part of the clothing worn by the horse-riding pastoralists that inhabited many of the areas to the north of the Silk Road. However, it seems likely that such practical footwear would also have been worn by travelers as well as individuals living more settled existences.

Exterior of a panel from the portable shrine

The interior panel of this shrine shows two of the most important moments in the biography of Siddhartha Gautama (died ca. 450 BCE), the historical Buddha. His birth, during which he appeared from his mother's right side and immediately stood and walked, is at the top. Tradition claims that the steps he took toward the four directions prefigure his future impact on world thought. The other figures shown are his mother, holding the branches of a tree as she gives birth; her two female attendants, standing to the right; and another figure, holding a cloth with which to swaddle the newborn, at the left.

Siddhartha's final transcendence, or *parinirvana*, is depicted in a separate scene at the bottom. The Buddha rests on his right side and is surrounded by monks and other devotees who are devastated by the loss of their teacher. The one exception, the monk sitting quietly at the front, is Sucandra, an early follower who understands that the final passing of Buddha Shakyamuni represents his escape from the inevitable cycle

Interior panel from the portable shrine

including eight bodhisattvas—beings of advanced spiritual development who chose to remain accessible to others in the phenomenal world—at the sides. Flying celestials, often symbolic of paradise-like realms, flit above the Buddha's head, and two additional bodhisattvas sit on lotus bases beneath the Buddha's throne. The small kneeling figure at the front may be the patron and user of the altarpiece. The two additional Buddhas with attendants at the top of the side panels illustrate the understanding that the cosmos is filled with numerous celestial Buddhas, an important idea in later Buddhist traditions. The four guardians of the cardinal directions and two additional terrifying protectors guard the sacred realm in the center. This shrine illustrates one of the earliest examples of mandalas—that of the Eight Great Bodhisattvas—the circular diagrams generally representing the cosmos, better known today in Tibetan art.

of birth and death and is therefore not a cause for grief. The missing other side of this shrine most likely also contained scenes from Siddhartha's hagiography.

Portable shrines were designed to close for transportation and open for prayer and teaching. Unlike stone shrines, which often had metal hinges, examples made of wood could be tied together using string or cord. The sandalwood example shown here, once painted green and red, consists of a central panel and two wings. The middle piece displays a crowned celestial (as opposed to the historical) Buddha—probably Vairocana—seated in meditation. He is attended by several other figures

Portable shrine with the Mandala of Eight Great Bodhisattvas

Many Visitors, Many Beliefs

China was home to a wide range of religions, many of which arrived there via the Silk Road.

Zoroastrianism Origin: Iran, ca. 500 BCE

Founded by Zoroaster (Zarathustra), this may have been the world's first monotheistic faith. It was once the religion of the Persian Empire, but it has been eclipsed by Islam; adherents number fewer than 200,000 today. Many religious historians think that Christian and Muslim beliefs concerning God and Satan, the soul, heaven and hell, the virgin birth, the slaughter of the innocents, the resurrection, and the final judgment were derived from Zoroastrianism. It reached China via the Silk Road by 500 CE.

Daoism and Confucianism Origin: China, ca. 550 BCE

These two religions were significant cultural forces in China, though they had little influence in other countries.

Daoism (or Taoism) started as a combination of psychology and philosophy but evolved into a religious faith when it was adopted as a state religion. At that time Laozi, its founder, became popularly venerated as a deity. The word *dao* can be roughly translated as "the path" or "the way." Along with Buddhism and Confucianism, Daoism became one of the three great religions of China. It currently has about 20 million followers and is centered primarily in Taiwan.

Confucianism is another blend of philosophy and religion that developed around the same time. It's based on the writings and teachings of Confucius, who dealt primarily with individual morality, ethics, and the proper exercise of political power. Confucianism is still practiced in China and other Far Eastern countries today, but mainly in combination with Buddhism,

A portrait of Confucius from a seventeenth-century Chinese scroll

Daoism, and traditional local practices. In this sense, current religious practice in China is a direct result of the kind of inter-faith mingling that took place along the Silk Road.

Nestorianism Origin: Turkey, ca. 430 CE

This sect of Christianity, which stressed the independence of Christ's divine and human natures, has all but disappeared today. It arose in what is now Turkey and spread along the Silk Road to the Middle East, India, and China.

This rubbing shows a section of the more than 1,200-year-old Nestorian stele, an engraved stone pillar erected in Xi'an in 781 and still standing today. With engravings from different time periods and both Chinese characters and Christian iconography—including a small cross at the top—the text records how "the illustrious religion" (Nestorian Christianity) spread to China in 635, under the reign of the Tang emperor Taizong.

Judaism Origin: Israel, ca. 2000 BCE

Still one of the world's great religions, practiced in every corner of the globe, Judaism emphasizes a belief in one God and fol-lows the tenets of the Old Testament. Jewish communities were scattered across Europe, the Middle East, and Asia—including China—during the Tang dynasty and afterward.

Manichaeism Origin: Iran, ca. 250 CE

Mani, the founder of this now-vanished sect, viewed himself as the last in a line of prophets that included Adam, Buddha, Zoroaster, and Jesus. Manichaeism held that the world was a fusion of spirit and matter and that the fallen soul was trapped in the evil mate-rial world and could reach the transcendent world only by way of the spirit. Zealous missionaries spread its doctrine through the Roman Empire and the East, along the Silk Road. Vigorously

A rubbing from a section of the Nestorian stele

attacked by both the Christian church and the Roman state, it disappeared almost entirely from Western Europe by the end of the fifth century but survived in Asia until the fourteenth century.

Islam Origin: Saudi Arabia, ca. 600 CE

Today, Islam has more than a billion followers worldwide—one-fifth of the world's population—and is considered one of the three major monotheistic faiths, along with Judaism and Christianity. (It might surprise you that less than 10 percent of today's Muslims are Arabs.) Islam, from an Arabic word meaning "peace" and "submission," teaches that one can only find peace by submitting to Allah in heart, soul, and deed. Islam arose around the holy cities of Mecca and Medina, and quickly spread into central Asia, India, and northern Africa.

Buddhism Origin: India, ca. 450 BCE

With more than 350 million followers worldwide, Buddhism is the world's fourth-largest religion, after Christianity, Islam, and Hinduism. It was founded in northern India by Siddhartha Gautama, known by followers as the Lord Buddha (though they believe in the existence of many Buddhas). It shares with Hinduism the belief in karma, dharma, and reincarnation, but, unlike Christianity, Judaism, and Islam, does not involve the worship of deities or belief in the existence of the human soul. Rather, it teaches selflessness and letting go.

Buddhism arose in India and Nepal and soon spread throughout Asia.

Following the Buddha

The popularity of Buddhism today comes from a legacy owed in large part to the Silk Road. Monks stationed along the routes preached to local populations that they, too, could escape life's suffering. They told local merchants that Buddha's mercy offered them protection on their perilous voyages. These messages were met with great enthusiasm, and by 500 CE, there were more than two million Buddhists in China, as well as sizable populations across the rest of Asia.

Royal Roots

Siddhartha Gautama was born to a royal Hindu family in what is now Nepal, around 450 BCE. After witnessing suffering, sickness, and death, the young prince abandoned his privileged life and began to travel, seeking guidance from spiritual leaders. While meditating under a fig tree in India, he attained nirvana, a transcendent state of being free from all suffering. For the rest of his life, he traveled the Indian subcontinent teaching others that they, too, could achieve nirvana by avoiding actions that produce pain and grief.

This painting of Bodhisattva Ksitigarbha is from a Mogao Cave temple.

This painting from 897 depicts Tejaprabha Buddha (Buddha of the Blazing Lights).

A JOURNEY OF 10,000 MILES

Late one night in 629 CE, a young Chinese monk named Xuanzang (602–664 CE) snuck past guards in Xi'an and set forth on an incredible journey to India, the center of Buddhist thought and practice. After sixteen years and 10,000 miles (16,100 kilometers) on the road, traveling over scorching deserts and perilous mountain passes, Xuanzang returned to Xi'an carrying hundreds of Buddhist manuscripts and relics. His detailed journals are to this day the only primary historical source of what life was like in parts of central Asia, India, and Southeast Asia during the period.

A depiction of Xuanzang's legendary journey

The Sounds of Xi'an

From a solitary flutist in the desert to grand orchestras in the palaces of Xi'an, musicians played all along the ancient Silk Road. Drumbeats rhythmically pounded in the distance, airy notes from wind instruments drifted by on the breeze, gentle tones from a bow drawn against strings, all punctuated by the sharp clash of cymbals—these made up the soundtrack of the region during the Tang dynasty. Indeed, music was a constant feature of life in Xi'an, enhancing rituals, telling stories, and bringing communities closer together through festivity and celebration.

Universal Language

Xi'an was home to musicians from across Asia—and the music of the city was the product of native and foreign influences. In particular, nations to the west sent musicians and orchestras to the Tang court, and Chinese musicians incorporated what they heard into their own rhythms and melodies. Further, some young musicians studied at specialized music schools in Xi'an, which taught foreign musical techniques and traditions.

Travelers on the ancient Silk Road may not have been able to understand one another's languages—but they could communicate and interact through music, which also served as a means to spread religious beliefs. Buddhist chants spread this way, for example, as did musical stories promoting Islamic values.

Instruments of Many Cultures

Musicians traveled from far and wide to perform in Xi'an during the Tang Dynasty, bearing a wide variety of instruments that had never before been seen there. The earliest stringed instruments had twisted silk for strings, which were scraped with bamboo strips to produce sounds. Of the many different kinds of stringed instruments in China, the modern *pipa* is best known. It originated in Persia, traveled first to India, and reached China by about 350 CE.

This figurine, from ca. 750, depicts a woman elegantly draped in silk and playing cymbals, an instrument commonly used in Tang-era musical performances.

LIVELY GATHERING PLACE

As we set out from Xi'an along the Silk Road, what will you remember of it? Take one more look back. Notice the camels clustered in loose groups outside the city walls and the colorful tents of the traders' camps, surrounded by bags, bundles, and provisions. Inhale one last time the heady perfume of the marketplace, piled high with spices from India, exotic foods, bolts of colorful silk, ceramics dishes and jars, and other precious goods. Wave farewell to the faces of many lands and cultures, and listen to the music of their languages and their mournful instruments.

Now, brace yourself for months of punishing travel along the harsh Taklimakan Desert road. Next stop: the lush oasis of Turfan!

A desert road leading to Turfan

Turfan

OASIS IN THE DESERT

The fertile lands of Xi'an give way to the harsh desert as our caravan wends its way to the north and west. Traveling on camelback, progress is slow and tedious through shifting sand dunes, some almost as tall as skyscrapers. As we look toward the horizon, we can see the brilliant red cliffs of the Flaming Mountains, so named because when the sun beats down on their flanks, they shimmer and dance as if on fire.

It's 1,550 miles (2,500 kilometers) from Xi'an through the Taklimakan Desert to the oasis of Turfan. After months of unrelenting heat and sand, its lush greenery and abundant water, supplied by runoff from the nearby mountains, are a welcome sight for thirsty people and camels alike. The incredible array of fruits and vegetables that grow here, thanks to ingenious irrigation systems that have been in use as long as anyone can remember, feed the local people and visitors, and the surplus will be traded along the Silk Road, reaching kitchens thousands of miles away.

HISTORY OF A GATHERING PLACE

Before we explore Turfan at its peak, let's travel back even further through time, before the dawn of the Common Era, and learn a little about its eventful history. As you can imagine, a fertile and arable spot such as this captivated the interest of people from many areas. In 107 BCE, the Chinese conquered the region and divided it into two kingdoms known as Nearer and Further Jushi. During the Han dynasty (206 BCE–220 CE), the city passed through the hands of the Xiongnu for a time, and experienced brief periods of independence. Until the fifth century, its capital was Jiaohe (a few miles west of today's Turfan).

In the fifth and sixth centuries, Turfan was ruled by a succession of Turkish tribes, but by the middle of the seventh century, the time of the Tang dynasty (618–907), the Chinese had reasserted their dominion. Alas, peaceful times there were few and far between. Throughout the seventh, eighth, and early ninth centuries, the entire region was a battleground for the Chinese, Tibetans, and Turkic people (ancestors of today's Uyghurs).

Under Tang rule, during the heyday of Silk Road commerce, Turfan's many inns served as gathering places for rest, refueling, and the exchange of ideas and goods. There is even evidence that the Sogdians, whom we will meet when we travel farther west to Samarkand, trafficked in pleasure there, supplying prostitutes to service the merchants passing through.

The Flaming Mountains

Jiaohe is one of the most well preserved examples of an ancient Chinese town.

A Uyghur painting from the eighth or ninth century

The Turkic Uyghurs held sway in the region for much of the time until their kingdom was taken over by Genghis Khan (ca. 1162–1227) and incorporated into the Mongol Empire in the twelfth and thirteenth centuries. Mongol control of Turfan lasted until the late fourteenth century, when the area again fell under contention, and smaller, often competing, polities ruled the region for centuries. Perhaps due to the near constant flux of power in Turfan and the surrounding areas, ties with the powerful neighboring Chinese dynasties, such as the Ming (1384–1644) and Qing (1644–1912), were complex, which at times led to crossed swords and problems with trade.

For instance, it is thought that the Mogul ruler Yunus Khan (1416–1487) came to power in Turfan in 1462 and unified Mogulistan—but he soon ran into difficulties with Ming China over trading terms. The Turfanians were eager to send lucrative "tribute missions" to China, but the Ming emperor felt that receiving and entertaining these missions involved more expense and trouble than they were worth. In 1465, he set up harsh restrictions, permitting only one mission into China every five years, with only ten members in any party. Frustrated, Yunus Khan declared war on China, but, not surprisingly, going up against the massive Chinese forces was doomed to failure.

Subjects remonstrate before a Chinese emperor.

By the late 1800s, Turfan consisted of two towns, each surrounded by walls. The Chinese town had a population of approximately 5,000 people, while the Turkish town, just about a mile (1.6 kilometers) to the west, had between 12,000 and 15,000. Today, once again unified as a county-level city in Turfan Prefecture (within the People's Republic of China), it retains its status as a kind of oasis in the midst of the inhospitable climate of the region. Turfan's population has swelled to more than 250,000 people who identify themselves as Uyghur, Mongol, Tibetan, Russian, Iranian, Chinese, and other nationalities—evidence that it remains the cultural crossroads it has been since ancient times.

CLIMATE AND GEOGRAPHY

The harsh cold-desert climate surrounding Turfan is a result of its location within a mountain basin, on the northern side of the Turfan Depression, at an elevation of 98 feet (30 meters) above sea level. Its summers are long and intensely hot—July temperatures average 103 degrees Fahrenheit (39.6 degrees Celsius). Winters are more moderate: during the coldest months, temperatures range from 10 to 28 degrees Fahrenheit (-12.1 to -2.3 degrees Celsius). Annual rainfall is extremely minimal, amounting to only about 0.62 inches (15.9 millimeters).

How then does Turfan remain verdant and productive of great quantities of beautiful fruits, vegetables, and other crops? The answer is in the combination of the very heat and dryness of its summers and the ancient system of irrigation known as the *karez* water system, which is still in use today. We'll look more closely at that man-made miracle soon.

TURFAN TODAY

Nowadays, Turfan is the official seat of the local prefecture, which includes one city and two counties, and has a population of some 540,000. Its location forms a hub linking southern and northern Xinjiang to each other and the surrounding countryside.

Much about Turfan is timeless. Its unique landscape, intense climate, and rich history make it as attractive to visitors today as it was in ancient times. It remains an oasis—a "garden city"— especially renowned for its vineyards. Because of this, the area surrounding Turfan is sometimes referred to as the Grape Valley. Visitors sampling the local wines are often surprised by the high quality and low prices. Cotton and melon fields can also be found dotting the countryside.

Lush greenery at the foot of the Flaming Mountains

Turfan's Ruins

Located at the northeastern edge of the Xinjiang Uyghur Autonomous Region, the area around the city of Turfan has long served as a meeting point for travelers and their goods on the Silk Road. The region has a complicated history, as it was controlled at different times by nomadic confederations, nomadic pastoralists, and settled populations—particularly the Chinese. The earliest records for the history of this part of the world are found in Chinese historical writings, which indicate that in the first century BCE Turfan was controlled by the Jushi, a people who lived in tents, had considerable knowledge of agriculture, and were proficient with bows and arrows.

The ruined city of Jiaohe (also known as Yarkhoto) is thought to have served as a capital for the Jushi before falling under the control of the Chinese in the first century CE. Arranged on a north-south axis, Jiaohe measured approximately 1,805 by 325 yards (1,650 by 300 meters) and contained numerous administrative and religious buildings. In the mid-fifth century, Gaochang, slightly to the east of Turfan, became the new administrative center. Measuring about 3 miles (5 kilometers) square, Gaochang was built using traditional central Asian mud bricks. It included a palace center as well as inner and outer complexes, both of which housed temples and other religious establishments.

A view of the ruins of the ancient city of Gaochang

Arguably one of the most important archaeological discoveries of the twentieth century, more than four hundred amazingly well-preserved mummies were excavated at sites near Turfan. They provide astonishing and unprecedented information regarding the inhabitants of the region from around 1700 BCE all the way to 200–300 CE. Naturally preserved by the dry climate, salty soil, and cold winters, the mummies include both Caucasoid and Mongoloid men, women, and children, which attests to the diversity of peoples who lived in this region. They were buried wearing clothing made of felt, wool, and silk. Some garments have plaid designs comparable to the tartans found in the Celtic world. Three of the female mummies were buried wearing long conical hats that are very similar to the witches' hats in European culture. A few have tattoos.

Others, such as a young Caucasian male with blond hair found at Yingpan near Lop Nor, have masks or cloths covering their faces—a burial practice also found in the ancient Greek world. The so-called "Yingpan man" was buried in a red woolen robe with yellow embroidery and a mask made of cloth (possibly hemp) over wood. A gold foil strip covered his forehead, and his head was rested on a satin pillow. The small pouch attached to the satin sash at his waist was probably used to hold medicine or aromatics. A necklace, a bow and several arrows, a glass cup, and a wooden comb were buried with him. Analyses, including study of the textiles, date this mummy to the second or third century CE.

The "Yingpan man" was excavated in 1998.

Mummies have also been found in a large cemetery at Astana near the ancient city of Gaochang. It contains approximately one thousand graves ranging in date from around 200 to 800 CE. Nearly half have been excavated. The graves, some of which were more richly appointed than others, contained well-preserved textiles woven in a variety of techniques; wheat and cotton seeds; dried pears, grapes, dumplings, and bits of dough; silk and paper flowers; and a large numbers of documents, some of which were written on recycled paper. These invaluable records include epitaphs detailing the biographies of the inhabitants of the tombs, inventories of graves' goods, and censuses as well as other administrative and economic reports.

Paper was also used to make some of the many tomb figures, including horses and oxen, found in the graves. The use of such tomb figures parallels Chinese traditions in which ceramic replicas of people and animals are placed in the tomb to serve the deceased in the afterlife (see page 50). One of the most spectacular figures found at Astana depicts a beautiful and stylish woman whose body is made of a wooden frame covered with paper. Her head is clay that was painted white. She wears garments that were popular in seventh-century China, including a sleeveless jacket over a green blouse;

This female figure was excavated from the tomb of Zhang Xiong and his wife.

a long, high-waisted skirt of alternating red and yellow stripes; and a light green shawl. The jacket is decorated with images of two birds facing each other within a pearl roundel, which are motifs derived from Persian imagery. Her belt is one of the earliest known examples of tapestry weaving. Her lips are painted red, her cheeks tinted pink (perhaps indicating the use of lipstick and blush), her eyebrows have been removed and redrawn, and a red floral design is painted on her forehead. She was found in the tomb of a Chinese man named Zhang Xiong and his wife, who was probably of a different ethnicity. They were buried around 688 CE.

During the eighth and early ninth century, the Turfan region and much of central Asia were controlled by Tibetans, who also briefly occupied parts of northern China. Around 840, the Uyghurs, who had been forced from their lands farther east, moved into the area and established an independent kingdom that lasted until the Mongol takeover in about 1280. Important and rare examples of Manichaean imagery were produced in the Turfan region under Uyghur patronage. Founded by the prophet Mani (ca. 216–276), Manichaeism was one of the many Gnostic (esoteric wisdom) religions that flourished in western and central Asia from the third to the seventh century. It has a complicated cosmology and focuses on the perennial battles

between the light/good and dark/evil. In
addition to paper manuscripts, some
with delicate paintings such as
an example found in a temple
in Gaochang, murals depicting
Manichaean themes are also
found in cave-temple complexes
at sites such as Bezeklik. Some of
these wall paintings were later covered
with Buddhist themes when Buddhism
became the state religion of the
Uyghurs kingdom. The Uyghurs, who
eventually converted to Islam, remain
the dominant ethnic group in the
Turfan region.

*This fragment from a manuscript
found in Temple A, Gaochang,
depicts Manichaean priests.*

Busy Marketplace

During its prime as a way station on the Silk Road, Turfan's markets came to life in the cool of the evening, offering exotic products from distant lands. Fashionable hats, elegant coats, and dazzling jewelry might seem out of place at a gritty desert market, but in fact the raw materials for such luxury goods, which were coveted as much for their style as for their practicality, were widely traded across Asia at the height of Silk Road commerce. Merchants brought expensive skins, feathers, and gems to the markets of Turfan, where eager buyers awaited to carry them off in all directions.

From Furs to Feathers

Hunters and trappers brought fox, rabbit, and ermine furs from the cold northern steppes and forests. Likewise, merchants from Persia (modern-day Iran) carried tough deerskins east for use in boots. Leopard skins from across Asia were particularly prized in China, but one physician warned, "One should not lie on one to sleep, for it will frighten a man's soul."

People all along the Silk Road used skins and furs as clothing, but Chinese merchants had a particular interest in animal tails for more symbolic purposes: Chinese military officers might wear them as badges of honor, or court officials as signs of their own authority. Indeed, animal tails had great symbolic power—Tang-era ceremonial processions included an officer in a carriage carrying a leopard tail pinned to a tall pole.

Colorful and dramatic, bird feathers were important trade items on the Silk Road as well. Vibrant pheasant and peacock feathers from southern Asia made their way north to China and central Asia, where they were used in military insignias, on hats and parasols, and in fans and brushes. In Tang China, a specially chosen officer was expected to arrange 156 peacock-tail fans at important state receptions.

Gems and Other Natural Treasures

Today, brilliant gems, ivory, and other gifts of the earth and its creatures fetch high prices, thanks to their rarity and special beauty. The same was true in Silk Road times, when traders carried such valuable objects great distances—from Afghanistan across all of Asia to China, and from Vietnam west to Persia. Political envoys frequently brought precious items—ranging from walrus tusks to emeralds—as gifts to foreign rulers.

Far left: A silk merchant that does business today much in the same way as merchants did during the height of the Silk Road.

Lapis lazuli, a brilliant blue stone that must have reminded anyone who held it of the crystal-clear water so precious in the region, was carried from northeastern Afghanistan and southeastern Tajikistan. Today those areas remain one of the best sources of the gem, still a favorite for jewelry of all kinds.

Fruits of the Vine

Walk into your local supermarket and you may well find French wines and Japanese pears. It might surprise you to learn that visitors to markets along the Silk Road—long before overnight shipping and refrigeration—could also choose from an array of foreign delicacies. As travelers moved along the trade routes, they introduced their own favorite ingredients and recipes to the foreign lands they found themselves in. Over time, the cuisine of one culture influenced that of another, as exotic edibles became familiar features on local menus. It's the same today, of course, as we all enjoy sampling Chinese, Indian, Japanese, or Mexican delicacies at one of the many ethnic restaurants that dot our communities, both large and small.

The fruits tended to come from desert oases such as Turfan, while the vegetables often traveled from central and northern Asia, and the nuts came from the Middle East. Great pains were taken to preserve the delicate edibles, but when that wasn't possible, traders came up with a different solution, sending seeds or young plants to foreign lands—often as tributes to powerful rulers. That way, even the most perishable food stuffs could grow and multiply in new soil.

Keeping fruit fresh under the desert sun is no easy task. Merchants in Turfan and other desert oases sometimes packed melons and other fruit in lead containers filled with snow and ice from the mountains—early precursors to our modern coolers and ice chests—before sending them along the Silk Road.

Right: A replica of a lead container used to transport fruit through the desert.

Far right: A fruit merchant

Tumeric

Mustard seeds

Dates

Exotic Flavors of Many Lands

Do you like salt on your popcorn or a nice spicy curry? People have long sought ways to spice up their meals and enhance the delicate flavors of meats, fish, vegetables, and other foods. It was no different along the Silk Road: salt, pepper, sugar, mustard, and other condiments were much desired everywhere from India to Persia to China. Many of these additives also had less familiar uses as drugs, perfumes, preservatives, animal repellants, cosmetics—even aphrodisiacs.

Beverages of Kings

Alcoholic drinks have been around longer than you might think. Even before the Silk Road, fermented beverages made from barley and rice were common in China. Grape wine, however, was rare. As the Tang empire expanded west during the 600s, Chinese traders brought home juicy grapes from Turfan and—even more important—the techniques for turning them into wine. Within decades, grape vines were growing in Xi'an, and grape wine could be found at important celebrations.

When the Tang emperor Muzong (reigned 821–824 CE)—known for his voracious appetite and taste for alcohol—first tasted grape wine from the West, he proclaimed, "When I drink this, I am instantly conscious of harmony suffusing my four limbs. It is the true Prince of Grand Tranquility."

It would be hard to describe the feeling better, don't you think?

Right: A vineyard in Turfan

Aromatics, Medicines, and Pigments

Today, it would seem strange to find medicines such as Epsom salts and aromatics such as frankincense at the same store. But in the ancient world, people made little distinction between substances that healed the body and those that enriched the senses. In fact, many of the same plant, mineral, and animal products were used as drugs in one place and as pleasing fragrances in another.

From China to the Middle East, people relied on plant, animal, and mineral products to cure illness or relieve pain. Markets in places such as Turfan offered new natural remedies from foreign lands, including cassia bark, gypsum, seaweed, sulfur, castor bean pods, human hair, rhino horn, and substances that were used medicinally, though today we think of them as recipe ingredients: saffron, mint, rhubarb, and the like.

One item sold along the Silk Road as a cure-all might seem pretty distasteful to a modern sensibility: the bezoar. A bezoar is an undigested mass of food and additional matter found in the stomachs of goats, cows, and other animals. In ancient times, these were believed to cure a variety of ailments. One Chinese doctor claimed that a bezoar "calms the heaven-soul and settles the earth-soul; it rids one of perverse goblins and puts an end to internal evils."

Not all ancient medicines seem quite so strange to Westerners as the bezoar. Ginseng, still popular all over the world for its healing properties, became known in China as the "divine herb" when it was introduced there during the era of the Silk Road. Carried to China from Korea and Manchuria, it was prized for its life-extending virtues—and it still is.

Today, some of us indulge ourselves with aromatherapy candles, incense, and scented oils, finding them soothing, mood enhancing—even spiritual. In ancient times, aromatics served

Bezoars

Frankincense

Saffron

Storax bark

an additional purpose: the pleasing aromas of burning incense and scented perfumes disguised the often unpleasant odors of daily life. Fragrances enhanced rituals and afforded the proceedings an air of magic and mysticism. Many aromatics originated in southern Asia—Indonesia, in particular—but could be found in marketplaces all along the Silk Road. Sought-after scents included sandalwood, ambergris, frankincense, myrrh, aloeswood, and storax bark.

White or crystalline camphor, taken from the wood of *Cinnamomum camphora* trees in southern Asia, emits a strong, pleasing odor. It was traded across Asia for a variety of aromatic and medicinal uses. In central India, the dead were sometimes cremated on a fire charged with camphor. Our most common use for the substance today is as a repellant to destructive, wool-devouring moths.

Bright, beautiful pigments made from minerals served a dual purpose in the ancient world. They were used to make vibrantly colored paints and cosmetics treasured by men and women wealthy enough to afford the luxury. Merchants at Silk Road markets offered these desirable minerals—including cinnabar, azurite, malachite, ocher, and carbon—for sale to eager artists and high-born ladies alike.

Silk has been used for an incredible range of things, including as canvas for paintings.

Textiles and Dyes

Trade in silk fabric gave the Silk Road its name, so let's pause for a moment to marvel at the tempting assortment of silks that could be found at Turfan's markets: sheer chiffons, lustrous satins, and elegant damasks, to name a few. Most favored of all were the exquisite Chinese silks, which merchants traded across Asia from Korea to the Mediterranean basin.

When we visited Xi'an, we learned the intriguing secrets of silk making. China was indeed the birthplace of silk—some ancient Greek and Roman scholars called China "Serica," or "Land of Silk." The many available varieties ranged from the simplest of weaves, intended for everyday use, to delicate, finely patterned cloth reserved for only the most important occasions. All of these could be found along the Silk Road, where they were traded by merchants who would bring them to countries throughout Asia and Europe.

KEEP THE CHANGE

Because silk is so much lighter and easier to transport than bronze coins, it was often used by merchants as currency. Even the Chinese government often paid officials stationed in remote Silk Road outposts such as Turfan in bolts of silk.

Natural Hues

In ancient times, the vibrant dyes used to color and decorate fabrics were made from substances found in nature. Even today, many textile makers prefer to use natural dyes made from plants (and sometimes animals) in much the same way they have been concocted for centuries. Since the plants and animals used to produce many of the most colorful and durable dyes live only in warmer climates, dyes from southern countries were usually traded to northern ones. There were several highly prized dyes:

Indigo. Indigo dye, originally derived from tropical plants, was popular across Asia during Silk Road times, and today synthetic indigo dyes are used to color many fabrics, including the denim beloved throughout the world for blue jeans. In Tang China, indigo was used most often in cosmetics.

Indigo

Lac. A resin secreted by many tree-dwelling insects, lac was collected from tree branches in the south and traded to east and west Asia. It was primarily used for dying fabrics, including silk, and as a cosmetic rouge to add a blush to ladies' cheeks.

Murex. This royal purple dye, found primarily in the Mediterranean, was made from a mucous secretion of a predatory sea snail. Even today, some artisans harvest the snails to obtain this rich, natural dye.

Beyond Silk

Silk may have been most prized, but it was by no means the only fabric traded along the Silk Road. Less flashy but nonetheless indispensable for their versatility and durability, fabrics made from a host of other natural fibers were common:

Wool. Sheep wool is familiar enough, but what about camel and yak wool? Central Asian herders followed a long tradition of sending textiles and rugs made from camel, yak, and sheep wool to marketplaces such as Turfan. Persian weavers—experts in making textiles from camel wool—passed the techniques across Asia, and soon other cultures were developing their own unusual kinds of "wool." Chinese and Tibetan artisans even made fabrics from rabbit and otter fur.

Cotton. Cotton was first domesticated thousands of years before the Silk Road, and fine cotton weaves were known across Asia. By 700 CE, Turfan, neighboring outposts in central Asia, and India in particular were producing cotton fabrics that became especially popular in China. In fact, the Turfanians had found a crop that thrived in its particular climate: the dry heat of the area lent itself to cotton plants, which are threatened by mildew in damper areas.

Linen, Hemp, and Other Textiles. Many other fabrics circulated along the Silk Road, including hemp, linen, and other cloth woven from vegetable fibers.

Left: A skein of wool yarn

Right: A cotton field in China

Shapes and Designs on the Silk Road

Trade in luxuries such as silk and metalwork spurred the movement of artistic shapes and designs along the Silk Road. Vessels and decorative motifs first created in one area of the Eurasian world would appear much later in another, and designs that originated in one medium were often transposed into other materials. Two spectacular ewers (or vase-shaped pitchers), one in metal that was excavated in China and another in porcelain that was made there, illustrate the extraordinary melding of forms and designs found in works of art produced at centers along the Silk Road. Both are in the shape of a vessel used in the ancient Greek world for pouring wine (known as oinochoe), which was also found later in Roman art, at times made of glass. Ewers of this type, typically made in bronze, silver, and possibly gold, appear to have been widely used in the ancient Persian world, particularly during the Sasanian Empire (224 BCE–651 CE). These Persian examples served as prototypes for ewers later produced in Afghanistan, Uzbekistan, and China from the fifth through the eighth century, as well as later Islamic pieces in pottery and metal.

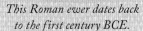

This Roman ewer dates back to the first century BCE.

The excavated piece, which was probably made around the area of present-day Afghanistan, was found in the tomb of Li Xian, an important general, who was buried with his wife in 569 CE in a tomb near Guyuan in the Ningxia Autonomous Region in northwestern China. Features such as the camel heads at the edges of the handle, the human head at the top, and the pearl-like decoration at the top and the bottom are often found in metalwork produced in Afghanistan and Uzbekistan during the fifth and sixth centuries, which is when this piece was likely produced. The six large figures on the body allude to the continuing importance of Greco-Roman art in this part of the world, which was first introduced with Alexander the Great's (356–322 BCE) conquest and later maintained due to trade with the Roman world. The three couples on the body of the ewer wear clothing and hairstyles reminiscent of those found in Greek and Roman art—they may represent figures from a saga such as the Trojan War. While it seems likely that General Li Xian did not recognize the imagery on this ewer, it was undoubtedly valued as a rare and highly treasured object that was buried with him so that he could enjoy it in his afterlife.

One of the most spectacular examples of a ewer expressing cultural crossovers is an eighth-century CE piece made in porcelain, a material first developed in China during the sixth to the eighth centuries. It has the same shape as the excavated ewer and is also decorated with pearl-like appliqués along the foot and neck. Pearls also define the roundels that fill the body—a textile motif shared by many cultures along the Silk Road. The unsteady, barely clad figures with wine jugs at their feet that fill the roundels may be allusions to Dionysus, the Greek god of wine, and/ or one of his followers. Like the Trojan War scenes discussed above, representations of a drunken Greek god in Chinese art are exoticisms. They were introduced via metalwork or textiles traded along the Silk Road, and not necessarily understood by the Chinese artist who made the porcelain ewer or the individual who used it. The palmlike designs on the lower part of the ewer are also Mediterranean motifs that traveled along the Silk Road and

The Greco-Roman influence on art in Afghanistan is apparent in this ewer.

This porcelain ewer illustrates the cultural exchanges along the Silk Road.

were incorporated into Chinese art. The use of appliqués, on the other hand, stems from the central Asian ceramic traditions, while the phoenix head that forms the cover and the sinuous dragon that serves as a handle are ubiquitous Chinese motifs.

THE MIRACULOUS *KAREZ* WATER SYSTEM

It's safe to say that Turfan and the other oases that welcomed weary travelers along the Silk Road could not have existed as the lush way stations they were without the complicated irrigation systems that allowed them to do what seems almost impossible: wring water from the desert. Some of the methods they used probably came from China, while others came from regions farther west. The system in use today is similar to that long known in the Persian world as a *karez*, which means "well."

Beneath desert sands, the underground canals of the karez carry water to fields miles away in the desert, transforming the barren landscape into a lush paradise. Since karezes rely on gravity to move the water underground, no pumps are needed, and because the flowing water is not exposed to the outside air, little of it is lost to evaporation. Karezes tap into water trapped in porous rock, water that comes from both rainfall and melting snow in the mountains. Even when Turfan and areas like it suffer from drought, the water carried there from the mountains is guaranteed to remain plentiful.

To create a karez, workers construct tunnels by punching shafts into the ground near the foot of the mountains, where the water table is shallow. They then connect the shafts underground

Above: Inside a karez

Right: An aerial view of the karez system

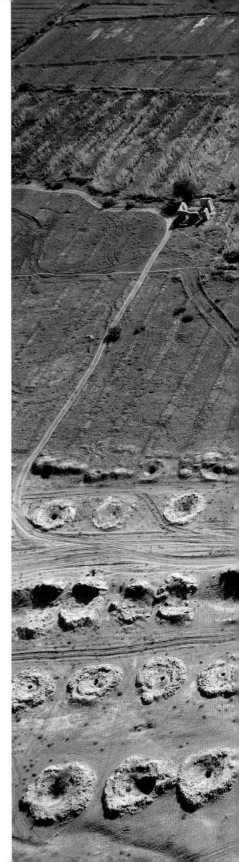

with a long tunnel. The shafts—or wells—are spaced every 30 to 115 feet (9 to 35 meters). They provide access for maintenance and allow people to draw water wherever they need it.

Karez tunnels are constructed so that the water travels down a slight, consistent slope. Karez tunnels run 30 miles (50 kilometers) or even longer! Small dams at karez outlets in turn create reservoirs to hold the water so that it might be used as needed for drinking, bathing, or irrigation.

The karez system is not the only one ever devised: many different irrigation systems have been used across Asia for millennia. But it is the one that seems to have lasted. Today, there are about 50,000 karez systems in Iran alone. Assembled end to end, they would stretch two-thirds of the way to the moon!

And more than 1,000 karez systems in the Turfan basin still move about 10 billion cubic feet (almost 300 million cubic meters) of water each year—enough to fill over 100,000 Olympic-sized swimming pools. Long lines of wells following each underground tunnel are visible from miles away.

FAREWELL TO TURFAN

Take one last drink of cool Turfan water and one last stroll through its twilit marketplace. Load up your pack camel with bundles of trade goods and provisions and plenty of water jars as we make our way back to the road—and we'll set out for the gated capital city of Sogdia known as Samarkand. At first we will travel mainly at night, to avoid the scorching daytime heat, but then you must be prepared to climb through the rugged and chilly passes of the Tian Shan range, keeping your eyes peeled for bandits along the steep, muddy trails.

A trail through the desert

Samarkand

CITY OF MERCHANTS

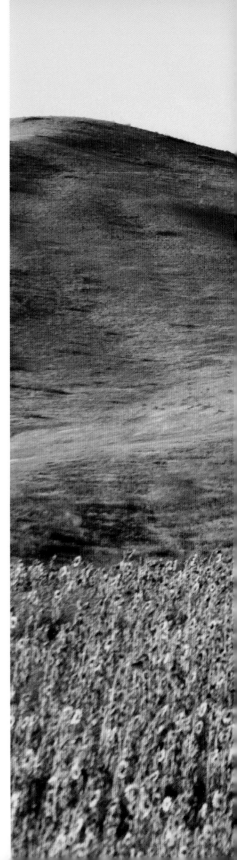

We've made it safely through the blustery Tian Shan range, and our caravan precipitously descends toward the green Fergana Valley, where we can take a break to enjoy sweet local fruit and fresh bread. (Our camels are more than content to munch on the abundant alfalfa.) As we approach the fabled city of Samarkand, its imposing gates swing open to welcome us. We've traveled another 1,600 miles (2,574 kilometers) since we basked in Turfan. We're now 3,000 miles (4,828 kilometers) from our starting point in Xi'an—the distance from New York to Los Angeles! Before we visit Samarkand's legendary merchants and sample their wares, let's learn a bit about the history and culture of this ancient city.

THE GEM OF THE EAST

Now the second-largest city in modern-day Uzbekistan, Samarkand is more than twenty-five centuries old, making it approximately the same age as Rome and Athens. Ancient Arab manuscripts refer to it as the "Gem of the East"—and when Alexander the Great (356–322 BCE) saw it for the first time he exclaimed, "I heard that the city was beautiful, but never believed it could be so beautiful and majestic." (Regardless of whether or not that love was requited, he would forcibly add it to his empire in 329 BCE.)

The city derives its lyrical name from the Old Persian word *asmara*, meaning "stone" or "rock," combined with the Sogdian *quand*, meaning "town." Founded around 700 BCE by the Persians, it remained a center of Persian-Sogdian civilization for generations. It was already the capital of Sogdiana, a province of the Persian Empire, when Alexander the Great conquered it, and the Greeks referred to it as Marakanda.

The Arabs took control of Samarkand in the eighth century CE, and it flourished as a center of trade, positioned strategically along a heavily traversed section of the Silk Road between China to the east and Baghdad to the west. (It forms the approximate midpoint of our own Silk Road journey from Xi'an to Istanbul, or what was known at the time as Constantinople.) In the ninth and tenth centuries, Samarkand emerged as a center of Islamic civilization, prospering under the Samanid dynasty of Khorasan (874–999) and then the Seljuks and the shahs of Khwarazm. The medieval era saw Samarkand at its peak, a fabulous city boasting impressive palaces and gardens overlooking paved, tree-lined streets. Its prosperous houses even had running water! Silk and iron industries flourished there, as merchants from India, Persia, and China converged and did

The Fergana Valley

business. Some of the finest paper that traveled the length and breadth of the Silk Road was also produced here.

This prosperous time would not last forever. In 1220, Genghis Khan (ca. 1162-1227) captured Samarkand and laid waste to it. Just a small number of local people survived—only to see their city devastated yet again only five decades later by another Mongol warlord, Khan Baraq. It took decades for Samarkand to recover—and yet, writing at the end of the thirteenth century, Marco Polo (who, granted, was more than a little prone to exaggeration) described it in his *Travels* as "a very large and splendid city."

REBIRTH

A renaissance for Samarkand came in 1370, when the Muslim conqueror Timur the Lame (or Tamerlane, 1336–1405) decided to make the besieged but beautiful city the capital of his empire, which extended from India to Turkey. Over the next four decades, he set about populating it with the finest artists and artisans from all of his lands. Under his reign, new palaces, mosques, and gardens were created, and Samarkand grew in population to 150,000 people.

It would be another fleeting period of glory: Timur's successors did not follow his lead, and under the Timurids, as they were called, the empire fell apart. Like Turfan, Samarkand became part of Mogulistan, and the city endured a succession of rulers with shifting allegiances. By the late sixteenth century, the Timurid dynasty was no more. Eventually Samarkand became part of the emirate of Bokhara.

Left: Alexander the Great depicted in battle
Right: A caravan outside Samarkand

MODERN TIMES

In 1868, Samarkand fell to a small Russian garrison of only five hundred men under the command of Colonel Alexander Abramov. It wasn't long before they themselves were besieged by the Abdul Malik Tura, son of the Bokharan emir—but Abramov prevailed, becoming the first governor of the area. In 1886, Samarkand became the capital of the newly created Samarkand Oblast of Russian Turkestan, and when the Trans-Caspian Railway reached the city two years later, it became the capital of the Uzbek Soviet Socialist Republic, before being replaced by Tashkent in 1930.

Samarkand Today

Having experienced precipitous ups and downs, Samarkand today is still a major center for the production of cotton and silk. Wine and tea are produced there, grain is processed, and other industries include metal products (as you'll learn, the city's tradition of fine metalworking stretches back to ancient times), tractor parts, leather goods, clothing, and footwear. It is the seat of Uzbekistan's state university as well as a variety of other institutions of training and higher learning.

A visit to modern Samarkand will carry you through a maze of narrow, winding streets to the Registan, its greatest square. The historic center of the city features some of the most remarkable monuments of central Asia, dating back to the late-fourteenth-century reign of Timur. His own mausoleum is capped by a ribbed and brilliantly colored dome, and the Bibi Khan mosque, featuring a turquoise cupola, was erected by Timur in memory of his favorite wife. The ruins of a sophisticated observatory built by his grandson, the great astronomer

Timur the Lame

The Bibi Khan mosque

Ulugh Beg, in the fifteenth century brings to mind Samarkand's early role in the scientific and cultural life of central Asia—but it also serves as a reminder that the battle between science and religion has been raging throughout the region's history. The observatory, housing what was at the time the world's largest and most sophisticated sextant, was destroyed by religious fanatics in 1449.

WHO WERE THE SOGDIANS?

We've learned that Samarkand was the Sogdian capital even before the Common Era, but who, exactly, were the Sogdians? Sogdiana (sometimes called Sogdia) has at different times included territories around Samarkand, Bokhara, Khujand, and Shahrisabz (formerly known as Kesh) in modern Uzbekistan. Its eastern Iranian people were among the ancestors of modern-day Uzbeks and Tajiks.

It was the Chinese explorer Zhang Qian, whom we have already learned about, who first carried news about the area back to China in the second century BCE. Soon after that, commercial relations between China and central Asia began to blossom, and Sogdiana formed an important central point.

At the height of Silk Road traffic, the Sogdians, perfectly situated geographically to act as intermediary traders between East and West, turned their energies to trade so thoroughly that the people from the ancient Chinese city of Khotan began to refer to all merchants as "Sogdian," no matter what their background or ethnicity. From their home base in Samarkand, the Sogdians became the dominant traveling merchants of the day, and their language (an eastern Iranian tongue closely related to Bactrian) became the lingua franca of the Silk Road. They played an important role in conveying culture, philosophy, and religion, including the tenets of Manichaeism, Zoroastrianism, and Buddhism.

The Chinese described the Sogdians as "born merchants," and, according to ancient documents, they learned their skills at an early age. Their reign as dominant salesmen lasted from the fourth century CE until the eighth century.

As late as the Middle Ages, the valley of the Zarafshan River around Samarkand retained the name Sogdiana, and Arabic geographers referred to it as one of the fairest districts in the world. Today, only the people living in one far-flung province of Tajikistan still speak a dialect of the Sogdian language.

The majority of Sogdians assimilated with other local groups, especially the Persians—modern Persian is peppered with numerous Sogdian words—but they will always be remembered as the most extraordinary entrepreneurs of the ancient world.

Sogdian art highlighting the riches of the culture

WHAT DO YOU DESIRE?

A stroll through Samarkand during Silk Road times offers glimpses of many coveted treasures. Are you seeking the finest in silk brocade? A sable coat, a packet of fragrant musk, or a smooth roll of cream-colored paper? Whatever you desire, chances are a merchant here can deliver it. These shrewd traders have built up a fortune buying and selling in distant countries, controlling a network of commerce that extends to India, China, and Persia. Welcome to the heart of their empire.

An Arab geographer named Muhammad ibn Hawqai, writing at the end of the first century, described the scene this way: "You cannot see any town or stopping place, or even desert, in the lands near Samarkand, without a convenient inn or stage-house for the accommodation of travelers, with everything necessary. I have heard that there are above two-thousand caravanserais or inns there, where as many persons as may arrive shall find sufficient forage for their beasts, and meat for themselves."

Previous page: Ulugh Beg observatory
Left: A spice merchant in a Samarkand market

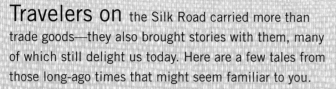

Stories of the Silk Road

Travelers on the Silk Road carried more than trade goods—they also brought stories with them, many of which still delight us today. Here are a few tales from those long-ago times that might seem familiar to you.

The Stonecutter Who Was Never Satisfied

In this Chinese folktale, many wishes come true, but happiness is still hard to find.

On a hot summer day in ancient China, a stonecutter worked long and hard swinging his hammer under the blazing sun. As he wiped the sweat from his brow, he thought to himself, "Surely the sun is the most powerful being in the world. I wish I could be the sun!" he cried. A fairy heard his wish and the sun he became.

Without wasting a second, he began to send hot sunbeams down to the land. It was wonderful to shine so bright! Then a cloud came drifting along and his light grew dim. How could that be? A cloud mightier than him! Now a white, fluffy cloud was what he wanted to be.

That wish too was granted and he became a cloud, happy just to float through the blue Chinese sky. Then along came the wind. It fluttered and whirled around him and would not let him be. "If I can't have my peace, then I'd rather blow free," he declared. "I want to be a fierce wind!"

The fairy listened and once more she offered help. Now he twisted and twirled. He teased branches and chased leaves. He dashed here and there, until he blew against a rock that stood in his way. He blew as hard as he could, but the stone didn't move. "If I were a stone," he thought, "no one would bother me. A stone is the best thing to be!"

So the fairy turned him into a big, heavy rock. He sat very still and watched time go by. Until one day a group of stonecutters came his way. They pounded away at him—just doing their job.

"Please, fairy!" he begged. "Being a stone is not what I want after all. From now on I want to be nobody else but me."

One last time, the stonecutter got his wish. He picked up his hammer and went back to work under the sweltering sun.

The Goose That Laid the Golden Eggs

This Greek story is one of Aesop's fables and was told in many lands along the Silk Road. The scenes shown here are based on a mural illustrating the tale, found near Samarkand in the ruins of a merchant's home.

There once was a man who owned a wonderful goose. Every morning, the goose laid for him a big beautiful egg—an egg made of pure, shiny, solid gold. Every morning, the man collected the golden eggs. And little by little, egg by egg, he began to grow rich.

But the man wanted more. "My goose has all those golden eggs inside her," he kept thinking. "Why not get them all at once?"

A depiction of The Lion and the Hare *from a book by Islamic writer Ibn Al-Mukaffa*

One day he couldn't wait any longer. He grabbed the goose and killed her. But there were no eggs inside her!

"Why did I do that?" the man cried. "Now there will be no more golden eggs."

The Lion and the Hare

This tale appears in an ancient Indian book of stories. In the time of the Silk Road, the book became very popular in the Middle East after it was translated into Persian, Arabic, and Hebrew.

In ancient times, a ferocious lion lived in the forest, killing without remorse. The other animals were terrified. To stop the lion's deadly hunts, some animals offered to provide him with food each day. Some animals would still die, of course, but the rest would live in peace. The lion agreed and enjoyed months of the easy life.

One day it was the hare's turn to present himself to the lion. Although small, the hare was very crafty. "Lion, lion," the hare cried out as he approached. "Help me, help me! Another lion is trying to eat me. But I am to be your dinner! You must stop him!"

Furious that someone was trying to steal his food, the lion demanded, "Take me to the thief. I will make him pay for this mischief!"

The hare and the lion made their way through the forest, eventually reached a deep well. There the lion looked down and saw his own reflection in the water. Thinking he had found the creature who tried to steal his food, the lion jumped down, ready to fight.

Alas, the lion never came out of that well, and the animals lived in peace from that day on.

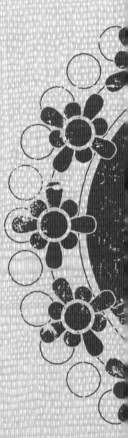

Paper: A Lightweight Revolution

According to legend, Islamic armies stole the secret of paper in 751, when they defeated Chinese forces at the Battle of Talas in central Asia. Several Chinese artisans were taken as captives and whisked off to Samarkand, where they founded the first paper mill in Islamic lands. Though this story is likely a myth, from that time on, Samarkand became famous throughout the Islamic world for its especially fine paper.

We may take it for granted today, or even claim we can do without it, but of all the treasures that moved along the Silk Road, none was more powerful than paper. This Chinese invention launched nothing short of a revolution in learning and literacy. Light, flexible, and inexpensive to make, paper became the ideal surface for recording ideas and made transporting and sharing them easier than it had ever been. As paper spread from China to the Middle East, it opened up a remarkable age of writing, reading, and learning.

Silk may have given the ancient trade routes their name, but paper gave them a brand-new and crucially important purpose.

A Sogdian letter

WRITING BEFORE PAPER

People have been writing for at least 5,000 years—much longer than they have been making paper. What did they write on before it was invented?

EAST AND SOUTH ASIA

Bamboo and Silk
Some of the earliest Chinese books were written on strips of bamboo, wood boards, or silk.

Talipot Palm Leaf
In India and Southeast Asia, writers once used strips cut from dried palm leaves to record their works.

WEST ASIA

Cuneiform Clay Tablet
Scribes of the ancient Middle East used a stylus made from a carefully cut reed to press wedge-shaped letters into clay.

Wood and Wax Tablet
Greek and Roman writers sometimes spread wooden tablets with a layer of wax, then traced letters in the wax with a stylus.

Parchment and Papyrus
In early Islamic times, the Qur'an and other sacred works were copied on vellum or parchment—animal skins that were scraped, soaked, and dried. Court records were kept on papyrus, made from the Egyptian papyrus plant.

A palm leaf manuscript depicting scenes from Buddha's life

In the Rough

Most of the paper we use today comes from wood pulp, but Chinese papermakers experimented with many kinds of plant fibers, including hemp, flax, and the bark of the paper mulberry tree. In central Asia and the Middle East, most paper was made from linen or cotton rags.

Ornamental paper was popular in China as well as the Islamic world. To prepare fine paper for writing, Islamic craftsmen coated the sheets with rice starch, polished them with a smooth stone, and tinted or decorated them with various dyes.

Papermaking, Step by Step

1. Shred plants or pieces of cloth and soak them in water.

2. Boil the plants and pound them to a pulp.

Early papermakers in central Asia used a papermaking mold that had two basic parts: a wooden frame and a flexible screen made of woven reeds. When the mold was dipped in the vat, the plant fibers formed a sheet on the screen. Then the screen was lifted off the frame and the sheet of paper was turned out to dry.

3. Mix the pulp with water in a vat. The tiny fibers will hang suspended in the water. Dip a paper mold in and lift it out. It will pick up a thin layer of pulp, forming a sheet.

4. Turn out the wet sheet of paper and press it to squeeze out the water.

5. Hang the paper to dry.

Paper, Pen, and Ink

As paper spread from east to west along the Silk Road, books became more bountiful than ever before. Chinese artists learned to smear ink on carved wooden blocks, which they used to print thousands of pages very quickly. When paper came to the Islamic world, a passion for reading and writing blossomed there, and Islamic scholars took the lead in the study of science, language, and literature.

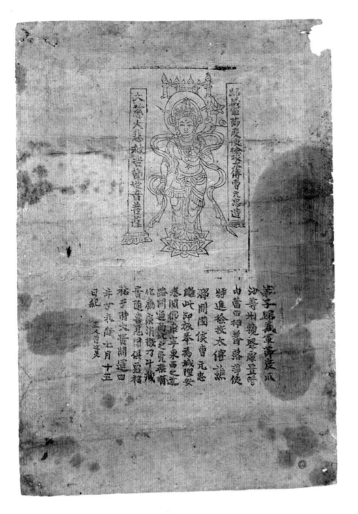

A woodblock print of the Invocation to Bodhisattva Avalokiteshvara

HANDCRAFTED

For many centuries, books were written by hand in the Middle East, not printed with wooden blocks as they sometimes were in China. But Islamic authors could still publish many books at a time. They would recite or read aloud, while a group of scribes took dictation.

In 1023, the Chinese government began block-printing money, using specially made mulberry paper to discourage counterfeiting. (This is not unlike our current practice of incorporating watermarks and other special features that are difficult to replicate into our paper currency.)

Silk Road traders also bought and sold goods using promissory notes, letters of credit, and other paper records to avoid carrying cash. And, as we learned earlier, silk itself was sometimes used as a lightweight but precious substitute for money.

Precious Uses

When paper was first introduced to the Islamic world, it was used for clerical tasks such as keeping tax accounts and other records. The arrival of paper also facilitated the blossoming of science and scholarship in the Middle East. It's safe to say that neither government, business, nor the arts could have been all that they were in the ancient world without the introduction of this lightweight substance—more precious than gold.

An early example of Chinese paper money

Though paper was quickly put to use in the arts and sciences, it is thought that Muslims were distrustful of paper to some degree. Their most sacred text, the Qur'an, continued to be transcribed on parchment and vellum for many years. Complete paper books dating back as far as 848 CE have been found—and it is suspected that thousands of paper manuscripts were produced around this time—but the Qur'an did not appear in this medium until the tenth century. The oldest paper copy on record is from 971–972 and was transcribed by the calligrapher Ali ibn Shadhan al-Razi. The script style in which the Qur'an was written also changed around this time, moving away from the artful *Kufic* scripts to a more contemporary cursive that was common in literary works. This change in style continued to transform the art of the written word in Islamic lands throughout the next centuries.

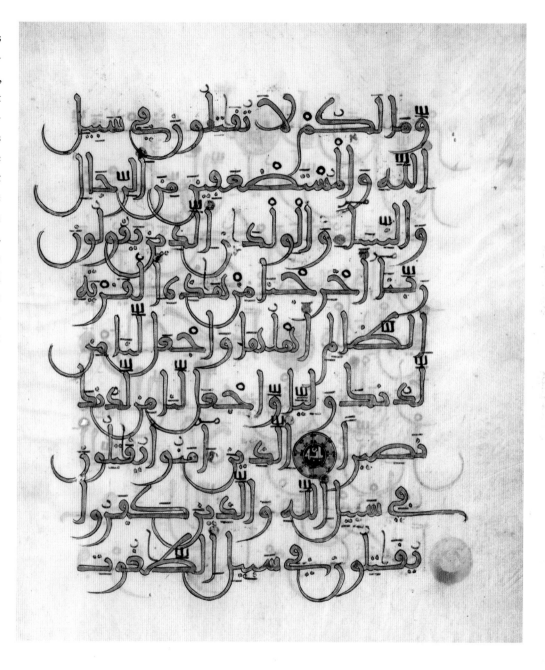

Left: Islamic scholars listen to a lecture in a library.

Above: A page of the Qu'ran on vellum

Paper, Printing, and Books

Of all the goods that traversed the Silk Road, it is paper—the most humble—that arguably had the greatest impact on global history. Chinese records mention the invention of paper by a court official named Cai Lun (ca. 50–121 CE) around 105. However, excavations at numerous sites in central Asia have yielded paper that can be dated earlier, and it is thought that this versatile material was actually first developed in south China sometime in the second or first century BCE. Prior to the development of paper, Chinese records were written on strips of wood and bamboo and pieces of silk.

The dark color of a fragment of a list of accounts found at Loulan, an ancient oasis town at the northeast edge of the Lop Nor desert, is typical of early examples. By the third century, paper made of mulberry bark and other fibers was lighter in tone. By the time of the Tang dynasty, paper was used for records and accounts, in textiles, for cosmetics, and to make kites (for entertainment and military signaling) and decorations such as flowers. Tang papermaking was highly specialized with different manufacturers producing papers of varying sizes and quality, and in colors such as white and green. After the fourteenth century, paper also became the primary medium for painting and calligraphy in China.

The dry climate around Loulan and other oasis centers helped to preserve documents including

A fragment of a list of accounts in Chinese from the Qin dynasty, excavated at Loulan, China

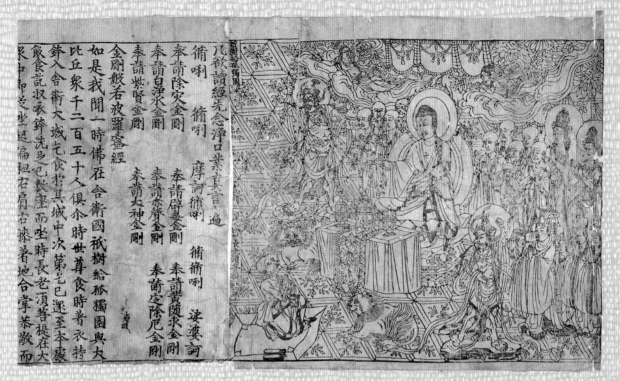

A woodblock print of the Diamond Sutra dated 868

letters, religious texts, and administrative records in some number. However, some of the most spectacular finds of the twentieth century—including a hidden library holding more than 10,000 manuscripts and paintings—were discovered within the cave-temples at the famed Buddhist site of Mogao near Dunhuang in northwestern China. Most of the paintings were on silk, but the records, which date from the fifth through the eleventh century, were written on paper in languages that included Sanskrit, Sogdian, Khotanese, Tibetan, and Chinese. These invaluable documents took several formats, including scrolls, books bound in a variety of fashions, and those folded in an accordion-like shape.

Some of the earliest examples of wood-block printing, which began in China around 700, were among the documents found in the caves at Mogao. The earliest

dated example of a printed book is a manuscript of the *Diamond Sutra,* a Buddhist text that was first translated into Chinese around 400. It consists of seven strips of paper bound together as a scroll that is over 17 feet (5 meters) long. As is often the case, the sutra has an illustrated frontispiece that shows a Buddha seated before an altar as he teaches an assembly of celestial beings and lay people. A colophon at the end has a date of 868 and indicates that a man named Wang Jie commissioned the piece to ensure blessings to his parents and to help spread the doctrine.

Buddhism, which stresses the making of images to gain merit, played a significant role in the development of wood-block printing in China. Monks used printing to quickly produce numerous texts and images, which were widely distributed for devotion, teaching, and

A leaf from an Arabic translation of the Materia Medica

protection. The first printing of the voluminous Buddhist canon occurred in China during the Northern Song dynasty (960–1126), and centers that produced a range of texts flourished during the Southern Song dynasty (1127–1279). Monks also helped to spread the technique of wood-block printing to Korea and Japan.

Around the middle of the eleventh century, the Chinese invented movable type. However, written Chinese consists of tens of thousands of characters that serve as words and therefore does not benefit from the use of this technology to the same degree as English or other languages that use an alphabet with a limited number of letters that are combined to form words.

Like the story of the invention of paper in China, that of its introduction to the Samarkand region in the mid-eighth century is apocryphal: the number of paper documents found at sites on the Silk Road makes it unlikely that Chinese prisoners—captured during the battle between Chinese forces and those of the Abbasid dynasty (750–1258)—introduced papermaking to Samarkand. This story, however, reflects the importance of paper in the Islamic world after the eighth century. It served a critical role in record keeping during the Abbasid caliphate that was based in Baghdad, as well as in earlier times when the Umayyad dynasty (661–750 CE) ruled from a center in Damascus.

Paper replaced earlier materials such as papyrus and parchment that were widely used throughout the ancient world. A market in Baghdad contained more than one hundred shops selling paper and books, and the availability of this material contributed to the development of science and literature that characterized early Islamic culture. For example, some of the earliest preserved records of the *Materia Medica*—a five-volume compendia of materials used in medicine, which was originally compiled in the first century CE by the Greek physician Dioscorides—are texts written and illustrated in Baghdad in the thirteenth century. The well-known *One Thousand and One Arabian Nights* was first recorded on paper in the ninth century.

Although the first paper versions of the Qur'an were produced in the middle of the tenth century, the text was written predominantly on more expensive parchment at this time. The earliest printed (as opposed to hand-

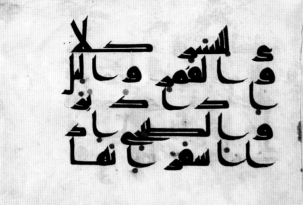

Two pages from a manuscript of the Qur'an transcribed during the Abbasid dynasty

written) Qur'an was produced in the sixteenth century. Jewish and Christian texts were also originally written on parchment.

Paper was introduced to Spain in the eighth century when the Islamic Umayyad dynasty was reestablished there after its defeat by the Abbasids. The first European document written on paper (probably made in the Islamic world) is a book of Catholic rites, which has been preserved in a monastery in Spain. By 1400, paper was produced in both Italy and Germany. After Johannes Guttenberg (ca. 1398–1468) developed a movable type in the mid-fifteenth century and printed a version of the Bible, bookmaking and literacy also became more widespread in Europe.

Evangelist Luke, Page from the Morgan Gospels, Northeast France, second half of the ninth century

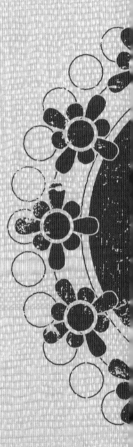

WAYS OF THE ROAD

The Sogdian merchants of Samarkand were experts on every aspect of trade along the Silk Road. Some put up the money for long-distance exchange. Some haggled in markets. And some acted as camel drivers and caravan leaders.

A single caravan might include peddlers, pilgrims, soldiers, guides, and many horses, mules, and camels. The leader had to be a special individual indeed, possessing great courage, skill at handling both animals and people, and vast knowledge of the trails and terrain.

After a long day's journey along the Silk Road, weary travelers could stop to rest at a caravanserai. In Islamic lands, these inns took on a standard form: rooms for sleeping and storing goods were arranged around an open courtyard where guests could water and feed their camels and horses. A thick wall with a guarded gate kept them secure from intruders. At a caravanserai, travelers of many cultures ate, bathed, traded goods, relaxed, and exchanged news and ideas.

> "Every two leagues along this desert road, small towers with water tanks have been built to collect rainwater . . . so that travelers may stop off and rest of awhile, out of the heat and cold. We saw great areas of shifting sands along the way. If anyone were to stray from the markers and wander into these shifting sands, there is no way he could come out again and he would surely perish."
> —Persian scholar and poet Nasir-i Khusraw, 1052

A night at a caravanserai is filled with the sound of music, laughter, shouting, poetry, and prayer. Clanging camel bells signal travelers that it is time for them to load up their bags as their caravan prepares to depart by night.

PACK ANIMALS

Miraculously well-adapted to the harsh desert conditions of central Asia and the Middle East, camels make ideal pack animals for travel along the Silk Road. These hardy creatures thrive on tough desert plants and can carry more weight than horses or donkeys—as much as 750 pounds (340 kilograms). And they need less water, too—a loaded camel can survive for many days without a drink if it has to.

HOW CAMELS COPE

Humps
Camel humps don't store water. They store fat, which provides energy when food can't be found.

Eyes
Bushy eyebrows and long, heavy eyelashes help protect camels' eyes from dust and sand.

Nose
Narrow nostrils can close to protect camels' noses from blowing sand.

Mouth and Stomach
Camels eat both grass and salty plants that grow in deserts. Their thick, tough lips can even put up with thorns.

Coat
A shaggy winter coat helps Bactrian camels stay warm in central Asia, where temperatures can drop to -30 degrees Fahrenheit (-34.5 degrees Celsius). Camel herders shear them and spin their hair into yarn to weave rugs, blankets, clothing, and bags.

Feet
Wide, padded feet help camels keep their balance on rocky paths and walk across the sand without sinking.

Camels and Caravans

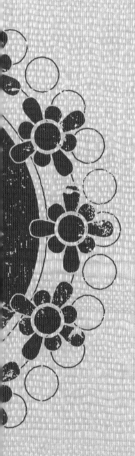

The popular image of a camel is a shaggy, Dr. Seussian sort of creature that can go days without water, traverse large stretches of desert, and subsist on a meager diet of scrubby bushes—all with a smile on its oversize head, contrasting with big sorrowful eyes and lashes to die for. In reality they are remarkable creatures, sturdy animals adapted to arid and marginal environments. They are also flea-bitten, tick-infested, smelly, and generally ill-tempered.

Camels are artiodactyls, meaning they have an even number of toes on each foot, and they are closely related to sheep and goats. Surprisingly, llamas, vicuñas, alpacas, and guanacos of the South American Andes and pampas are in the same family as camels, and fossil evidence demonstrates that camels originated in North America. The two varieties of Silk Road camels are the one-humped North African and Middle Eastern dromedaries, or Arabians (*Camelus dromedarius*), and the two-humped central Asian Bactrian camels (*Camelus bactrianus*). Both species were first domesticated more than 4,500 years ago and have played an integral role in the development of civilization in Asia, Africa, and the Middle East as a food source and, more importantly, as vehicles that transport goods, people, and ideas across vast expanses of land.

Most of the camels on the Silk Road were Bactrian camels, although farther west dromedaries were encountered more frequently. One bas-relief carved into the pink rock walls of the abandoned Nabatean city of Petra (in present-day Jordan) shows a caravan of dromedaries entering the city. Similar artistry from eastern Asia almost always depicts Bactrian camels. The Bactrian camels are sturdier caravan animals, although stockier and not as fast as their one-humped cousins. They were originally domesticated from central Asian stock, and today only about a thousand truly wild Bactrian camels are left. These can be found primarily in the mountainous Trans Altai borderlands of Mongolia and China.

The secret to the camel's ability to penetrate some of the most hostile areas on Earth is due to a series of physical and physiological adaptations. Several of these are ways in which camels conserve water, which is an extremely limited resource in deserts. A camel's water supply is regulated by their peculiar ability to lose up to 30 percent of their body weight to dehydration. This would kill most animals. Camel dehydration can be quickly recharged by drinking prodigiously—up to thirty gallons in ten minutes. Hydrating at this level would also kill most animals through water intoxication.

Other specialized water conservation features include nostrils that reabsorb water while exhaling and a urinary and digestive system that is extraordinarily efficient in recovering almost all metabolic water. When stressed, camel urine is thick and goopy, and their fecal matter is so dry that it can be burned as fuel almost immediately. They even have specially shaped red blood cells that are

An Arabian camel (left) and a Bactrian camel (right)

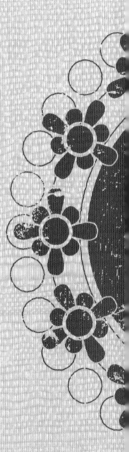

adapted to withstand severe dehydration. But even with all of these evolutionary tricks, camels still need water at least every five days to stay in good health, and the caravaneers' knowledge of the location of wells and springs to water camels on the Silk Road was paramount.

It is commonly believed that camels store water in their humps. This is a myth, and a bad one at that.

Camel humps are made of fat; camels with firm humps are well-fed camels, and camels with saggy humps are poorly nourished. While some water can be generated by the metabolism of these fat deposits, it is minimal. Camels can eat almost anything, as their lips, palates, and tongues are tough enough to allow them to consume even the spiniest and thorniest desert bushes. Camels can also healthily endure a range in body temperature of about 10 degrees Fahrenheit—compare that to how we feel with a slight fever. Their paws (a Mongolian delicacy on their own) are huge and allow for the even distribution of weight on unsteady sands.

Exquisite pottery figures and tomb paintings, especially from Tang-dynasty China, preserve the look and feel of the loaded camels and their masters, passengers, and pullers. From these we can tell that both people and cargo were a mixed lot. There are camel pullers and grooms with decidedly non-Han Chinese faces, probably representing Sogdians, Kashmiris, Uyghurs, and Mongols; some of these have even been called Semitic. While some ancient documents written in Hebrew have been found in

central Asia, recent scholarship concludes that these were probably Persian peoples of a sort. Records of business transactions concerning the camel loads have been found, sometimes written in the form of "contracts" on wooden sticks, which would be broken when the contract was fulfilled. Most provide pretty dry information, such as lists of mercantile goods and payments given or received.

Few historical records of the inner workings of camel caravans exist. Curiously, one of our best views of an ancient camel caravan comes from Owen Lattimore's early twentieth-century classic *The Desert Road to Turkestan.* Here, in 1926, Lattimore details one of the last camel caravans as he accompanied it across the Gobi

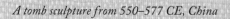

A tomb sculpture from 550–577 CE, China

Working camels in present-day Mongolia

in China from Hohhot (in Inner Mongolia) to Xinjiang. Lattimore portrayed the life on a caravan as excruciatingly hard and hierarchical, with strict codes of respect and place enforced by cruelty.

Although probably not as large as the caravans in antiquity, these twentieth-century caravans marched sometimes by day and other times by night depending on weather conditions, topography, and fear of bandits—as has been the case throughout the history of the Silk Road. Each camel could carry up to 750 pounds (340 kilograms) of cargo; however, to preserve the health of the animals, they often carried much less. On caravan, camels were arranged in strings, called files, that included up to twenty-five animals each guided by a separate camel puller.

In addition to the cargo, each camel had to carry supplies of its own fodder in case requisite feed could not be found along the routes. Each day the caravan would cover a length, or stage, of 10 to 25 miles (16 to 40 kilometers) depending on the terrain and how recently the camels had been watered. As tough as these animals were, historical sources indicate that camels needed to rest for two months after a desert trek before they were physically recovered and ready for their next journey.

Today Bactrian camels are still a very vital part of nomadic society in Mongolia and parts of China. They are raised for their fur, milk, and even meat. A large male Bactrian can produce several kilograms of camel hair in a year. This hair, which wild camels shed in the springtime, is necessary as insulation from the harsh central Asian winters. Domestic camels are shorn in the spring, and their winter hair is packed in bales. Camel-hair traders purchase the bales, and the hair is sent to Milan and Paris to hit the runways and racks as fine couture.

Sogdian Splendor

The merchants of Samarkand and other Sogdian cities lived richly on the profits of long-distance trade. Accordingly, their lavish houses were beautifully adorned and designed for entertaining. Like the princes who ruled the country, these businessmen delighted in displaying their wealth. Beautiful murals lined their walls, depicting historic scenes and heroic battles.

The Sogdians were widely admired for their talent as entertainers. In China, they sparked a craze for a dance called the Sogdian Swirl. "The movements of this dance are as swift as a whirlwind," remarked a Chinese writer in the 700s.

Silver and Gold

The mountains of central Asia contain rich deposits of lead sulfide, a mineral that often bears traces of silver. Ancient miners extracted the silver by crushing the ore and then smelting it in a clay container. Most of the lead melted and was skimmed off, leaving the precious silver—which has a much higher melting temperature—behind in the bowl.

The markets of central Asia bustled with workshops where artists shaped metal into decorative forms, often combing several metals into highly decorated vessels. Both Persian and Sogdian artists excelled at the craft of shaping beautiful objects from these precious metals. Caravan merchants, in turn, traded these gleaming vessels for silk on the borders of China, and for furs, honey, and amber near the Caspian Sea.

Metal workers often decorated their creations with hunting scenes, and weavers used many of the same designs when creating patterns for silk.

In this fresco scene a dragon attacks Rustam, an ancient Persian hero. Rustam has cut the dragon twice with his ax, and flames spurt from the wounds.

This marble panel depicts Sogdian dancers.

Left and below: The same ferocious animal forms a repeating pattern on the silver and gold platter below and this silk brocade.

Small treasures, such as silver bowls, were valuable and easy to transport, making them ideal for trade along the Silk Road. As gold and silver wares were traded to distant countries, foreign rulers developed a taste for the Persian style they represented. This is but one example of the way fashion and style moved along the trade routes, one culture influencing another, until evidence of this intermingling could be found at the farthest reaches of the Silk Road.

Coins—the most efficient trade good of all—were minted by Persian, Sogdian, and Arab rulers and circulated in the markets of central Asia. Much of the silver used to cast these coins came f̶͟͞ t̶o̶ t̶h̶ ̶n̶o̶r̶t̶h and east of Samarkand.

FAREWELL TO SAMARKAND

Drain your cup and finish the delicacies on your plate— it is time to thank our gracious hosts and leave the prosperous homes and markets of Samarkand. As the city gates close behind us, we direct our camels west once more. Before too long, we'll find ourselves wading across the Amu Dar'ya, one of the longest rivers in central Asia. Next, we'll trudge along the northern rim of Iran's Great Salt Desert, remaining vigilant for scorpions and snakes. Finally, we must hike up and over the rugged passes of the Zagros Mountains and down into the plains of Iraq.

We're headed straight for Baghdad—the capital of the Islamic world!

Far right: The Amu Dar'ya

Our long and trying journey has carried us thousands of miles from the imperial city of Xi'an. At long last, we enter its western rival: Baghdad, City of Peace. Its gleaming palaces and fragrant gardens look down on the Tigris River; foreign goods arrive daily by ship via the Persian Gulf as well as by camel caravan, all under the watchful eye of an illustrious group of Islamic rulers known as caliphs. With their patronage, the city has blossomed into a remarkable center of learning—a meeting place for scholars, scientists, and philosophers, and a storehouse for both new and ancient knowledge of many lands.

We are fortunate to be visiting Baghdad during its golden age of the Abbasid era (750–1258). Over its long history, the city, located strategically at the narrowest point between the Tigris and Euphrates rivers, has often been besieged, invaded, laid to waste, and resurrected. All too often—and even to this day—Baghdad has found itself in the line of fire between factions warring over land, resources, and religion.

Our visit predates the strife and conquest that will tear it apart repeatedly and tarnish its reputation as a capital of enlightenment—but before we wander its artfully laid out, circular streets, let's take a brief look at Baghdad through the ages.

"GOD'S GIFT"

There are various theories as to the etymology of Baghdad's name, but the most widely accepted is that it comes from the Persian words *bag* (god) and *dad* (given). Another explanation is that it derives from the words for "garden" and "giver." Either way points to the natural beauty of its locale on a vast plain bisected by the river Tigris.

Baghdad was founded in the year 762 CE by the Abbasid caliph Al Mansur (709–775), who said of the site, "This is indeed the city that I am to found, where I am to live, and where my descendants will reign afterward." Though the site was merely a small village at the time the caliph began plans, it took only a few decades for it to become one of the wealthiest cities in the known world. Its rapid growth was undoubtedly aided by its ideal location, which afforded control over the trade routes along the Tigris to the sea and throughout all of Asia.

In its earliest days, it was known by several names: Madinat al-Salaam (City of Peace) and "the round city," because that is exactly what it was: its design featured nested circles surrounding the main mosque and Golden Gate Palace, the residence of the caliph and his family. During the

The tomb of Sheik Ma'ruf in the desert of Baghdad

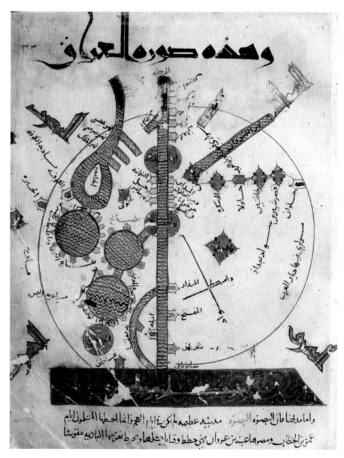

Above: This page from Animals and Their Uses *by Baghdad physician Ibn Bakhtishu depicts Aristotle and Alexander the Great*

Right: An eleventh century map of Iraq

Abbasid era, Islamic scholars studied geometry and the mysterious symmetry of the circle. (Like Greek and Indian scholars, they recognized that the world was a sphere.) Marble steps led down to the river's edge, and its many parks, gardens, villas, and promenades gave the city an unparalleled elegance.

To construct his dream city, the caliph hired engineers, surveyors, and builders from all over, along with many thousands of workers. The final design included two concentric rings of residential, commercial, and military structures inside the city walls, in a nod to traditional Persian design. This circular plan was in sharp contrast to the Greek and Roman cities of the day, which were constructed as squares or rectangles with streets intersecting at right angles. (Today's Washington, D.C. is built on the circular model, while New York City reflects the Greco-Roman-style grid plan.)

Brief Glory of the Abbasids

The Abbasids believed themselves to be the progenitors of two traditions—the Arabian-Islamic and the Persian—and they attempted to reconcile the two in their way of life. While the city's design and architecture reflected Persian influences, the caliph demonstrated his dedication to his Islamic identity by building the House of Wisdom, where ancient texts were stored, studied, and translated.

Scholars from across the Abbasid Empire traveled there, and in this way Greek and Indian ideas and innovations were introduced to the Arabic world. For much of its golden age, Baghdad was probably one of the largest cities in the world, with more than a million inhabitants—possibly even two million—at its peak. (Today's Baghdad supports a population of more than seven million.)

Right: Al Mansur
Far Right: Abbasid Palace

One Thousand and One Arabian Nights: Stories for All Time

You have surely heard of the tales of Scheherazade known as *One Thousand and One Nights* or, simply, *The Arabian Nights*. The fifth Abbasid caliph, Harun al-Rashid, appears in some of these tales, many of which take place in Baghdad during its golden age.

The work as it exists today was collected over many centuries, and in addition to stories from the caliphate era, it includes tales that can be traced back to the folklore of Persia, India, Egypt, and Mesopotamia. The framing story of Scheherazade was probably drawn from a Persian work, which itself incorporated Indian influences.

The oldest Arabic manuscript of *One Thousand and One Nights* that we know of dates from the fourteenth century, though scholars generally agree that the story was created around the ninth. The first European version appeared in the early eighteenth century, translated into French by Antoine Galland from an Arabic text, but it included a number of stories not in the original manuscript—including some of our favorites today: "Aladdin's Lamp," "Ali Baba and the Forty Thieves,"

Harun al-Rashid

عا عبش ليلس و

Aladdin and the genie

and "The Seven Voyages of Sinbad." Although different versions of the book include different tales, what they all have in common is the framing story, which can be synopsized as follows.

A Persian king, Shahryar, discovers evidence that his new bride has been unfaithful to him. In his anger, he has her executed and declares all women to be unfaithful creatures. He begins to marry a succession of virgins, only to execute each one the morning after their wedding night. Eventually, the king's vizier cannot find any more virgins in the kingdom—but the vizier's own daughter, Scheherazade, offers herself, and her father reluctantly agrees.

On the night of her marriage to the king, Scheherazade begins to tell the king a story, but she doesn't end it— forcing him to postpone her execution so that he might hear how the fascinating tale concludes. The next night, she imparts the ending—but begins a new story, forcing the king to postpone her execution yet again. This continues for 1,001 nights.

The stories included in the volume are meant to represent the various tales told by Scheherazade to the king. Some editions contain only a few hundred "nights," while others compile a full 1,001 stories. They include historical tales, love stories, tragedies, comedies, poems, horror tales—even erotica. Many depict djinns (genies), magicians, and fantastic places, intermingled with real people and geography. Within this rich collection can be found early crime fiction, science fiction, and satire, along with many tales that hinge on fate, destiny, and coincidence. The historical caliph Harun al-Rashid, his vizier, and his court poet are the protagonists of many of the most beloved and oft-repeated tales, despite the fact that they lived some two hundred years after the fall of the Abbasids, the time during which the framing story is set.

Full of surprising plot twists and what we think of as modern literary devices (foreshadowing, stories-within-stories, allusions to other works, etc.), these enthralling tales have truly stood the test of time. They've been retold as contemporary novels, adapted into films, plays, operas, radio broadcasts, cartoons, and television shows, and have even been used as the basis for video games. (You have probably seen Disney's 1992 animated adaptation *Aladdin* or some version of "The Seven Voyages of Sinbad," the story that has most often been dramatized for the screen in many countries.) As recently as 2008, a brand-new English translation was published by Penguin Classics in three volumes, including the standard text, the so-called orphan stories of Aladdin and Ali Baba, and an alternative ending to Sinbad.

But what of Scheherazade? Different versions of *One Thousand and One Nights* have different endings. In some, Scheherazade asks for a pardon; in some, the king decides not to execute her out of love for their children; and in others, something happens to distract the king from his plan—but they all end with her life being spared. In the world of this influential and immensely enjoyable book, a great story well told is as important as life or death.

Scheherazade with King Shahryar

Invasion and Destruction

The Abbasids' reign in Baghdad was not destined to last. Internal political struggles led to the relocation of the capital to Samarra and the loss of the western and easternmost provinces. Periods of domination by the Persian Buwayhids and the Seljuk Turks gave way to invasion by the Mongols in 1258, under the leadership of Hulago Khan (1217–1265), a grandson of Genghis Khan. This cataclysmic siege, known as the Sack of Baghdad, destroyed the caliphate once and for all, along with much of what the Abbasids had created. Most of the city's inhabitants were massacred, its irrigation system was destroyed, and large sections of the city were razed to the ground.

The Mongol emperors of Iran, known as the Il-Khanids, held the city for nearly a century and a half. In 1401, Baghdad was again sacked, this time by Timur (or Tamerlane, 1336–1405)—and again, the population was massacred almost to a man.

In 1534, Baghdad was conquered by the Ottoman Turks, enemies of Persia, and the city continued to move away from its prosperous beginnings. It remained under Ottoman rule until 1917, when it was captured by the British during World War I. Keeping the local Arabs and Kurds at bay, the Brits established the Kingdom of Iraq, under British control, in 1921. It is safe to say that Baghdad never again rose to the heights it reached as an elegant center of commerce and learning in the eighth and ninth centuries.

Modern Times

Iraq was granted formal independence in 1932 and even more autonomy in 1946, although it remained under a monarchy installed by the British. In 1958, the Iraqi army deposed King Faisal II in a bloody coup, achieving true independence for the first time in centuries.

The Mongols invading Baghdad in 1258

Above: A page from al-Khwarizmi's Algebra

Previous page: The Ramadan mosque in modern-day Baghdad's skyline

During the 1970s, as the cost of oil soared, Baghdad prospered and invested in its infrastructure, modernizing its water system and building new highways. But with the Iran-Iraq war of the 1980s, money was diverted to the military, and civilian casualties mounted. Since then, every decade has brought new conflict—beginning with the Persian Gulf War in 1991, through the 2003 American-British invasion that deposed Saddam Hussein, right up to the present.

The ongoing occupation of Iraq, along with harsh sectarian violence, has resulted in a decimated and beleaguered city, divided into distinct, mutually hostile zones: a large Shia city to the east of the Tigris and a smaller Sunni city on its west side. The river that inspired Abbasid caliph Al Mansur to build his shining city some 1,250 years ago now serves as a battle line between warring factions in an occupied land.

"I mention Baghdad first of all because it is the heart of Iraq, and, with no equal on earth either in the Orient or the Occident. . . . It stretches out on the two banks of those two large rivers, the Tigris and the Euphrates, and watches commercial products and staples flow to it on land and on water. . . . One would think that all the goods of the earth are sent there, all the treasures of the world gathered there, and all the blessings of the universes concentrated there."

–Arab geographer Ahmad al-Yaqubi (died 897 CE)

A TIME OF DISCOVERY

Now, let's travel back to Silk Road times, and the role Baghdad played in the development of the world's knowledge and culture. Whenever you look at a map, gaze at the stars, or take down a phone number, think of Baghdad in its golden age, when brilliant scholars in this booming city studied geography, engineering, astronomy, and mathematics. They made advances that can still be felt every day. Great minds from many lands gathered at the House of Wisdom—an enormous library and center of learning.

The study of mathematics was of great interest to scholars at the time. They poured over Indian books on the subject, which used a set of ten symbols to represent numbers—rather than letters of the alphabet, as had always been the way in Baghdad and Rome. In the early 800s, mathematician Muhammad ibn Musa al-Khwarizmi (ca. 780–850) wrote a book on doing math using the system developed in India. Three centuries later, it was translated into Latin. Eventually, people all over Europe followed al-Khwarizmi's example, and switched to the "arabic" numerals we use today.

Another great mind changed the practice of medicine forever. Muhammad ibn Zakariya al-Razi (865–925) had a theory about health and cleanliness, long before the discovery of microbes and bacteria. It is said that he chose the most sanitary location for a Baghdad hospital by hanging meat in different neighborhoods to see where it took longest to rot. A firm believer in logic and close observation, al-Razi wrote some two hundred manuscripts, from a pamphlet on toothaches to a medical handbook that was used in Europe for hundreds of years.

Doctors evaluate a patient.

INNOVATIONS FOR ALL TIME

"He who travels in the search of knowledge, to him God shows the way of Paradise."

—attributed to the Prophet Muhammad

ca. 860

Arab scientist Yaqub ibn Ishaq al-Kindi discovered how to isolate alcohol and wrote more than one hundred formulas for perfumes.

964

Persian astronomer Abd al-Rahman al-Sufi wrote a ground-breaking guide to the stars.

ca. 1000

Al-Hasan ibn al-Haytham, a scholar who worked in Baghdad and Cairo, experimented with the physics of light.

1025

Persian physician Abu Ali al-Husayn ibn Abd Allah ibn Sina (known as Avicenna in the West, 980–1037 CE), wrote *The Canon of Medicine,* which was used as a medical textbook in Europe until the seventeenth century.

ca. 1070

Persian poet and mathematician Omar Khayyam made advances in algebra and geometry.

ca. 1100–1200

Scholars translated scientific works from Arabic into Latin, setting the stage for the European Renaissance.

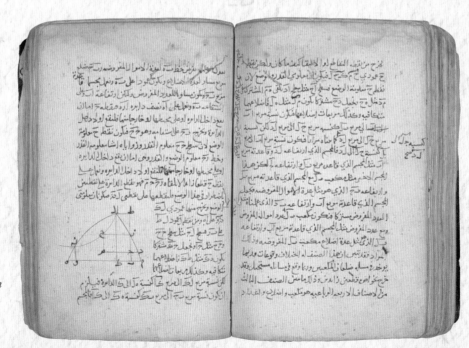

A manuscript page from mathematician Omar Khayyam

The Stars and Beyond

The night sky was an object of great fascination and study in Silk Road times. Both Chinese and Islamic astronomers pictured the heavens as a sphere that rotated around Earth. To represent the position and movement of stars, they arranged the constellations around a globe—the way they would look to someone outside the celestial sphere. These celestial globes were made in India and Pakistan.

But the most useful device in an Islamic astronomer's tool kit was the astrolabe: a guide to the night sky and a form of calculator that helped chart space and time.

By measuring the position of the sun and stars, they could precisely tell the time of day or night and predict the moment that the sun would rise in the morning. The idea for the astrolabe was adapted from the Greeks, but Islamic scholars refined it and added many new features to make it more versatile. According to one early expert, this fabulous instrument had a thousand uses in all.

A celestial globe

Ingenious Devices

Among the most dazzling treasures of the Abbasid age were its inventions: machines that performed all kinds of tasks, from serving drinks to telling time. Many of these extravagant inventions were devised simply to entertain wealthy patrons, but the best of them had an impact far beyond entertainment.

One particularly ingenious Islamic craftsman, court engineer Abu al-Izz ibn Ismail al-Jazari (1136–1206), devised plans for fifty miraculous gadgets, including faucets that spewed wine and water, mechanical peacocks, and a robotic musical band. In around 1200 CE, he designed a water clock, known as a clepsydra, which employed a water wheel to control the flow through the clock and measure the time.

Left: An astrolabe

Above: Scholars using an astrolabe

The constellation Orion from Abd al-Rahman's manuscript

Great Books on Many Subjects

In 964, the Persian astronomer Abd al-Rahman al-Sufi combined Greek, Persian, and Arab knowledge of the sky into a single work, *The Book of Fixed Stars*. Organized by constellation, his work described the position, color, and brightness of more than a thousand stars and served as an astronomical handbook for many centuries.

Islamic scholars translated many Greek works into Arabic, including a groundbreaking book on medicinal plants, *Materia Medica*, by the Greek physician Dioscorides (ca. 40–90 CE).

In the 900s, Arab and Persian geographers traveled the Islamic world and drew maps to illustrate what they learned. The maps they made encouraged people to travel by helping them navigate the landscape and anticipate distances, the time it would take to get where they wanted to go, and the impediments they might encounter along the way.

A scene from a thirteenth century Arabic version of Materia Medica

GLORIOUS GLASS

Not every innovation of the ancient world was mechanical or scientific. We've already read about silk from China and paper from Samarkand. Glittering glass from the Middle East traveled to distant markets along the Silk Road as well. Traders had to use resourceful creativity in transporting the fragile material.

It's not hard to figure out why glass captivated the fancy of all who could afford it, just as silk did. Prized for its beauty, glass catches the light in a unique way, flashing crystal clear or sparkling with color. When molten, it can be shaped as no other material can: with a puff of air.

The art of blowing glass developed around 100 BCE, but it reached new heights under Islam. Glass from Baghdad and other Islamic cities traveled over the trade routes toward China, where it was treated as the rarest of jewels.

Most glassworkers in the Middle East used the same basic technique to create glass objects, and it varies little from the method used by glass artists today. They gathered molten glass on the end of a blowpipe and then breathed into it to form a bubble. The bubble could be reheated and reshaped to make different vessels.

After glassblowers finished the shaping, they then used a variety of techniques to decorate a glass object. These included blowing it into a mold so the surface was impressed with a design; dribbling a stream of molten glass on top of the surface; cutting, grinding, or filing away parts of the glass to create a design in relief; etching (scratching) a pattern into the glass with a diamond or other hard stone; reheating the glass and pinching a pattern into it with tongs; and trailing a second color of glass over the first, then combing through the colors to create a pattern and rolling the entire piece smooth.

Since transporting the fragile glass pieces was such a tricky business, glassmakers often exported lumps of unworked glass, called cullet, instead. After shipment, these lumps of glass were reheated and blown, or fashioned into jewelry. By buying cullet, a craftsman could skip the first few steps of glassmaking, which call for an extremely hot furnace—and therefore large amounts of fuel.

Above: Glass from Palestine around the first century BCE

Right: A glass bottle dated between the seventh and early eighth century

GLASSBLOWING, STEP BY STEP

Above: Glassmaking today is often done the same way as it was in the first century BCE.

Next page: Glassmaking depicted in manuscript

Glass is made from a mixture of minerals that are melted and blown.

1. Mix three basic ingredients:
Sand containing large amounts of silica.
Soda ash, often made by burning plants known as saltwort or glasswort. (The Arabic words for these plants are the roots for our terms *soda* and *alkali*.)
Lime obtained by heating limestone.

2. Heat the mixture in a furnace to about 2,500 degrees Fahrenheit (1,370 degrees Celsius). Lower the temperature, then dip the end of a blowpipe into the molten glass, capturing a large bead of glass.

3. Blow into the pipe to form a bubble.

4. Shape the bubble by rolling it against a flat surface or pinching, pulling, or cutting it with other tools.

Other Roads

From today's perspective, it is easy to think of the ancient Silk Road as one long superhighway spanning Eurasia. This is naive. Instead of a single track, the Silk Road was a spiderweb of topographically defined routes that crisscrossed the continent and interconnected with trade routes from the Arabian Peninsula, Oceania, and even northern Africa. In places, the routes ended in port cities where goods were transferred to boats and ships for open water, coastal, and riverine transport. The routes were both north–south and east–west, and at their nexuses where major caravanning tracks met, important commercial centers developed where goods, ideas, religion, language, and bloodlines were exchanged. There were dozens of small, specialized routes as well. On some scale there was a trade route for every individual commodity trafficked on the Silk Road. Each one is deserving of a book detailing its rich history and the relationship between the goods and the people who traded in them.

One of the major elements of Eurasian commerce was the spice trade. In antiquity (and still today in most of Asia), spices were used as a condiment, preservative, and taste enhancer for food, but they also had important medicinal and cosmetic uses. Because most spices are native to

particular geographic areas and many are perishable, their transmission across vast distances was a grueling but profitable undertaking. Cinnamon and black pepper are good examples of this trade. Both are known far into antiquity (cinnamon was used by the ancient Egyptians for embalming, and black pepper was a favored condiment of the Romans) and are indigenous to the Indian subcontinent, Sri Lanka, and the Moluccas islands.

Many spices, especially aromatics like sandalwood, made their way northward through the Himalayas to become important components of Chinese civilization in the form of incense and medicinal unguents. It can even be argued that the Western taste for spices fueled the age of exploration, as the spice trade was a primary motivation for the voyages of Magellan and Columbus. Found in many of the same areas, bird feathers including the peacock's and the iridescent plumage of the kingfisher; gems such as rubies, sapphires, and diamonds; and sea products like turtle shell, pearls, and coral also made the journey north, and in some cases westward, along with the spice caravans.

Another southerly trade route was the tea road emanating in Yunnan province in southwestern China. The tea plant is indigenous to this area of China that straddles the Burmese border. Although tea drinking has a long history in

Peppercorns

Tea being weighed

China, it did not become fashionable among the northern people until the late Tang (618–907) and early Song dynasties (960–1279). Especially during the Song, large organized trading routes from Yunnan extended to the Tibetan highlands where a large-scale tea culture had developed. Much of the payment for tea appears to have been made in the form of horses—consequently this route has been called the "Tea and Horse Caravan Road."

Routes across and down from the steppes, a belt that extends from Mongolia across Eurasia, were also important thoroughfares for mercantile goods. The steppes were the home of pastoral nomads who had horse cultures that took advantage of the ideal geography for caravanning. Across these areas people moved freely, and goods could be easily transported across great distances.

The forests of Siberia were teeming with game and provided a rich source of furs supplied by tribal hunters. Everything from ermine to minks, tigers, and arctic foxes trimmed the gowns, boots, and hats of the fashionistas from Persian, Arab, central Asian, and Chinese noble houses. Other materials that moved southward were metals, such as silver, which formed the basis for the

great tradition of Sogdian and Scythian metalworking. Amber from as far away as the Baltic Sea reportedly has been found in China. Even much of the rich tradition of ivory carving practiced by the Chinese has its roots in the frozen Siberian steppes. While elephants are usually associated with warm southern climates, the permafrost is a rich repository of fossil elephant ivory. Carbon 14 analyses of contemporary Silk Road ivory carvings have shown them to be fashioned from extinct Pleistocene mammoths as opposed to modern Asian or African elephants.

The enduring legacy of the Silk Road is that it is difficult to define. Often viewed simply as a unidirectional east–west conduit for silk that lasted through the medieval period, it was clearly so much more. Its origins extend back thousands of years, and much of it (even though many of the goods have changed) remains vital today. The variation in goods accumulates to almost anything anyone would ever want. The routes themselves went everywhere across all sorts of climates and geographies, and the modes of transportation varied accordingly. Even from the American alpha-consumer standpoint, the cosmopolitan sorts of treasures that could have been found at the market in some dusty central Asian desert town over a millennium ago would be awe inspiring.

Mongolia steppes

GRACIOUS LIVING

Stylish people in early Baghdad enjoyed serving drinks in delicate glass containers, just as many hosts do today. Islamic artists created glassware in dozens of colors and patterns to grace elegant homes.

And what did they drink from these beautiful vessels? Wine, of course. Although the Qur'an advices believers not to drink wine, many in early Baghdad did. The Muslim physician Abu Ali al-Husayn ibn Abd Allah ibn Sina recommended it—in small doses: "It is of sharp flavor, like a father's advice, but useful also; permitted to the intelligent, forbidden to fools. Is it the fault of wine if a fool drinks it and goes stumbling in the darkness? Religion allows it to the wise, if reason forbids it to asses."

A ninth-century goblet with the inscription: "Blessings from Allah to the owner of the goblet. Drink!"

The Art of Writing

For artists in early Baghdad, words were shapes as well as sounds. Islamic artists turned the curving shapes of the Arabic alphabet into an elegant art form, and the language blossomed into a visual art as scribes made graceful copies of the Qur'an. But calligraphy soon moved beyond the page. With the spread of Islam, the flowing letters began to wind around serving dishes, embellish clothing, and splash across doorways, ceilings, and walls.

Calligraphers made ink by mixing gum arabic, made from the sap of acacia trees, with lampblack—soot that was traditionally scraped from inside mosque lamps. But special documents might be written in gold or other colors of ink, ink that sparkled with ground glass, or even invisible ink!

A stone slab engraved with elegant Kufic calligraphy

THE BEGINNING OF ISLAM

The Islamic religion is based on the teachings of Muhammad, a merchant from the Arabian city of Mecca who lived from around 570 to 632. Muhammad became the leader of the Arab people in the early 600s, after receiving a series of messages that he accepted as the word of God, or Allah.

Muhammad recited these revelations to others, and after his death, his followers gathered them into a book that became known as the Qur'an, or "recitation." Early Qur'ans were written on fine-quality parchment, or vellum. Calligraphers used a bold, angular Arabic script called Kufic to write them, which was said to have originated in the city of Kufa, in what is today's Iraq. With the help of the Qur'an, the new religion of Islam spread—and Arabic calligraphy spread along with it.

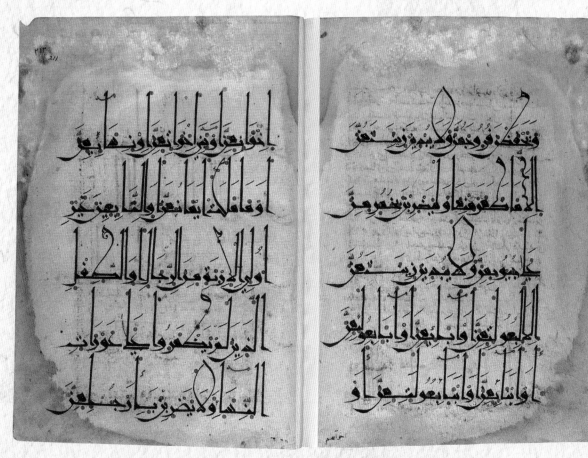

A Qur'an written in Kufic calligraphy

This serving dish is from between the tenth and eleventh centuries.

Islamic potters often decorated their wares with blessings or lines of verse. The Arabic inscription on the bowl pictured here reads, "The miser sees only one path to wealth.... generosity is a quality of the people of Paradise."

Early Arab poets saw similarities between the letters of a beautifully written alphabet and the features of an attractive woman. The letter ا (*aleph*), or *A*, was compared to a woman's tall, slender figure. The letter ن (*nun*), or *N*, was said to be like a lady's lock of hair, its dot forming the mole on her cheek.

By the early 1200s, Baghdad was a virtual paradise for readers and writers, with an enormous stationer's market, more than one hundred bookshops, and thirty-six public libraries. One magnificent library belonged to a college called the Mustansiriya Madrasa. Its reading rooms provided paper, pens, and oil lamps so students could copy the texts and make books of their own. Each student also enjoyed free tuition, room, board, and medical care, as well as a gold coin for every month of his stay.

ONWARD FROM BAGHDAD

As enlightening as our stay in the gracious and scholarly city of Baghdad has been, it will soon be time to press onward toward Istanbul (or Constantinople, as it was known in Silk Road times). But before we go, take a moment to reflect on all that we have discovered here. Baghdad truly is a special gathering place, where the wisest and most curious from far and wide come to study, experiment, innovate, create beautiful works of art and craft, and share ideas and traditions. There may never be another cultural center quite like the Baghdad of the caliphs—but we are fortunate to have so many extraordinary objects, ingenious devices, and lovingly created books and documents to help us envision the glorious place it once was.

The next leg of our journey will carry us nearly 1,000 miles (1,609 kilometers)—to Istanbul and the seas beyond!

Extensions

ISTANBUL AND THE SEA

Istanbul:

CITY THAT SPANS CONTINENTS

Our long journey from Baghdad at last brings us to Istanbul—or, as it was known in Silk Road times, Constantinople. This is the last city on our colorful journey from east to west—we've traveled more than 5,000 rugged miles (8,000 kilometers) since leaving China and arrived in a city whose strategic location has made it one of the most significant capitals throughout history, as well as one of the most turbulent.

In its glory, Constantinople was the largest and richest city in the eastern Mediterranean, commanding the trade routes throughout much of the Mediterranean basin. It remained the glittering capital of the Greek-influenced Byzantine Empire for more than a thousand years, from the fifth through the fifteenth centuries, exerting both cultural and economic influence over the entire Mediterranean region. But this impressive metropolis—the world's only city to extend into two continents—was conquered and sacked many times over by a succession of regimes enamored with its geography, if not its wealth, people, and culture. Its violent history spans the rise and fall of the world's most storied empires.

EARLIEST TIMES

What we now call Asian Istanbul was probably inhabited as far back as 5,000 years ago, but it wasn't a city until the Greeks arrived in the seventh century BCE. As the story goes, the Greek King Byzas chose the location after consulting the Oracle at Delphi, who told him to settle in a spot overlooking the Straits of Bosporus. In his own honor, Byzas named the city Byzantium.

By the first century CE, the city had become part of the Roman Empire. In 330, Emperor Constantine the Great (ca. 280–337) set out to turn it into a glittering center, complete with

A map of Constantinople showing its ideal location

BYZANTIVM NVNC CONSTANTINOPOLIS.

Palazo di Constantino Imperatore

PERA

ARSENALE

MAHOMET AMVRATES

MAHOMET BAIAZETES SELIM SOLIMANO SELIM AMVRATH OTTM

impressive monuments in the Roman style. In 330, he declared it the capital of the unified Roman Empire and—like his predecessor—renamed it for himself: Constantinople.

For a time, the city grew and prospered, but upon the death of Emperor Theodosius I in 395, his sons divided the empire, and Constantinople became the capital of the Byzantine—or Eastern Roman—Empire. As such, it took on a more distinctly Greek identity.

Because it was situated at the crossroads of two continents, on a peninsula called the Golden Horn at the entrance to the Black Sea, Constantinople became a center of trade, culture, and diplomacy. After an antigovernment revolt destroyed much of the city in 532, it was rebuilt, its many new buildings and monuments surpassing the old ones in their beauty and durability. It was during this period that the city's most revered extant structure took shape: an archetypal example of Byzantine architecture and culture known as the Hagia Sophia. With it, Constantinople became the center of the Greek Orthodox Church.

The Hagia Sophia: Living History

"The church is singularly full of light and sunshine; you would declare that the place is not lighted by the sun from without, but that the rays are produced within itself, such an abundance of light is poured into this church."

—Prokopios, sixth-century Greek historian

Istanbul's greatest landmark has so far led three lives: as a Christian church, a mosque, and today a museum.

Erected atop the first of the famed seven hills of Constantinople, at the tip of the peninsula surrounded by the Sea of Marmara, the Bosporus, and the harbor known as the Golden Horn, the Hagia Sophia (which means "Holy Wisdom") was built between 532 and 537 by Justinian I (483–565). As you can imagine, significant structures had existed on this glorious site previously. In fact, the Hagia Sophia was the grandest of three churches built on the site since 360—the most recent having just been razed, during the violent Nika riot (a combination sports and political riot). Immediately upon quelling that revolt, Justinian commissioned the large and imposing church to unify the faithful and reassert his authority as emperor.

Christian iconography and architecture were at the core of Constantinople's transition from a Roman city into a Byzantine one, and the Hagia Sophia was the most potent symbol of the new order. Prior to its construction, the dominant architectural form for churches was the basilica—a rectangular building with a long nave leading to the altar and a pointed, timbered roof. The Hagia Sophia was instead designed around a grand dome, presenting a difficult technical challenge at

Looking up inside the main dome of the Hagia Sophia

the time. (The initial dome partially collapsed during an earthquake in 557 and took five years to reconstruct. The new dome, taller and braced with forty ribs, again had to be partially rebuilt after more seismic activity in the ninth and tenth centuries.)

As the main imperial church, attended regularly by the emperor and his family, the Hagia Sophia was a center of spiritual life in the city. Along with the Hippodrome (an arena used for chariot races and other attractions) and the Imperial Palace complex, it occupied much of the prime triangle of land bounded by the Bosporus, Marmara Sea, and the Golden Horn; it is the only one of the three structures to survive in anything akin to its original form.

With the brief exception of the period of Latin occupation following the Fourth Crusade in 1204, the Hagia Sophia remained the center of Eastern Christianity from 360 until the Ottoman era began in 1453. At that point, it began its second life when Sultan Mehmed II (1432–1481) converted it into a mosque and ushered in an era of Islamic worship in the holy structure. It remained the central mosque of the Ottoman capital until its secularization under the Turkish Republic in the mid-twentieth century. A period of study, restoration, and cleaning of this precious landmark began in earnest in the 1940s and continues to this day, as tourism to the region and common interest in the structure has reached an all-time high. It is currently open to visitors as a cultural and architectural museum.

Turmoil and Turnover

The extraordinary location and wealth of Constantinople was to be its undoing many times over during the next several centuries, as it was besieged successively by Persians, Arabs, various nomadic peoples, and during the Fourth Crusade,

A cross-section plan of the Hagia Sophia

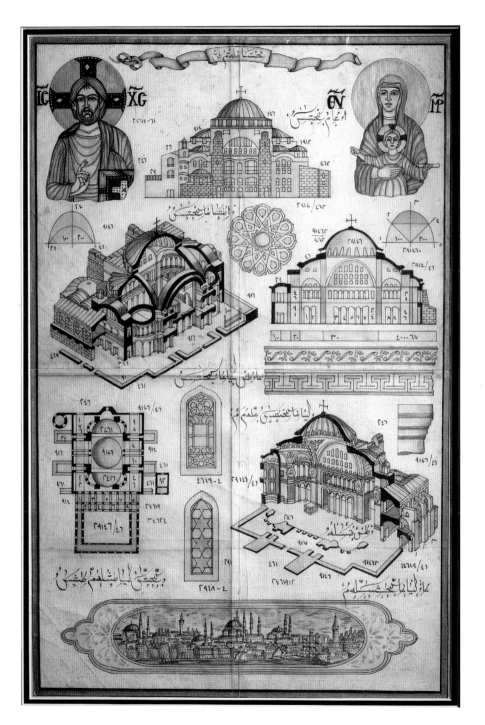

which desecrated the city in 1204 and turned it into the center of the Catholic Latin Empire. With the exception of a brief period in the 1100s, when Byzantium staged a remarkable military, financial, and territorial recovery, the area was continually buffeted, the art and architecture of many centuries looted, or worse, destroyed.

The city suffered and deteriorated as it became a battleground in the competition between the Catholic Latin Empire and the Greek Orthodox Byzantine Empire. Attacks by Mamluks, Arabs, and Persians were also near constant. Its economy collapsed, its population declined, and it became even more vulnerable to attack. In 1261, Constantinople was recaptured from the Latins by the empire of Nicaea, and returned to the Byzantine Empire—but during that same period, the Ottoman Turks were systematically overtaking a number of cities surrounding it, effectively isolating it from its neighbors. They were setting themselves up nicely for the invasion that was to come.

A Port of Trade

Although Rome was a key destination for the Chinese silk and other goods that traveled the Silk Road during its first few centuries, beginning around the fourth century, Constantinople thrived as an important destination in its own right for riches from the East. Even as it declined and fell into the hands of the Ottoman Turks a thousand years later, the wealth of the city was renowned, and its location ensured that it would always play a pivotal role in long-distance commerce. And as it experienced rebirth as Istanbul and again took its place as a great capital, it grew ever more central in the exchange of both goods and ideas.

The Hagia Sophia

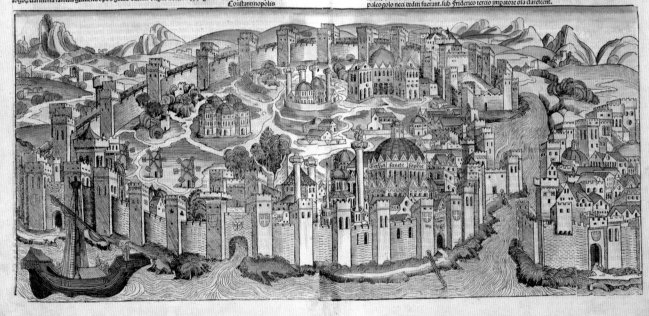

A third-century Greek historian named Polybios stated that he could not imagine a location better suited to control trade from the Black Sea into the Aegean, thus playing a key role in providing Greece with such essentials as honey, wax, grain, and even slaves. He called it "a site that is absolutely the most advantageous for safety and prosperity in the world as we know it."

A depiction of Constantinople's key location as a trade hub

Left: The siege of Constantinople during the Fourth Crusade

The Last Stop on the Silk Road— Byzantium and the West

The Western Roman Empire fell in 476 CE when the last reigning Latin sovereign, Romulus Augustus, was deposed by the Germanic king Odoacer (435–493). In the West, this is the beginning of the so-called Dark Ages, a time when Europe was thrown into centuries of intellectual and economic poverty from which it would not emerge until the Renaissance. Conspicuously, the decline of the West roughly corresponds with the advent of the glory days of Silk Road trade. So, if it wasn't Europe, where were the final markets for precious luxury goods transported over thousands of miles?

Misconceptions abound about Europe and the Mediterranean during these times. Recent archeology shows that trade through the continent was much more substantial than previously considered. Remnants of silk garments have been found in Roman burials in Britain and in a sixth-century grave in Germany. Images of Buddha, also from the sixth century, that originated in the Swat valley in the Gandhara area of northern Pakistan were buried in Viking funerary pits near the village of Helgö, Sweden.

A Buddha from the Viking funerary pits

Between the fifth and fifteenth centuries, the Byzantine Empire was one of the largest and richest states in the world and was the western terminus of the Silk Road. It exerted broad influence over southern Europe, northwestern Africa, Anatolia in Turkey, the Levant (or the eastern Mediterranean), and farther reaches of the Middle East. Its capital city of Constantinople was called the "Queen of Cities." Geographically, Constantinople was both easy to defend and the nexus for regional trade routes. The city itself was filled with monuments like the Hippodrome that reflected the city's Roman and Hellenistic past as well as magnificent buildings like the great church of Hagia Sophia, which was the largest cathedral in the world for nearly a millennium.

The Byzantine Empire was a huge market for silks, jewels, and other exotica transported along Silk Road conduits. Exotic spices—such as pepper, turmeric, and cinnamon—that made their way to Mediterranean ports were quickly incorporated into local cuisine. Yet while the capital was the destination for many of the goods, it was also the transit point through which

A Byzantine mosaic from the Hagia Sophia of an empress

trade flowed. During this period Byzantines controlled much of the Mediterranean, inheriting control of eastern ports from the Romans, who had inherited them from the Phoenicians, Persians, Nabateans, and others. The cities of Antioch, Tyre, Acre, and Alexandria were important ports, and it was in these places that goods were loaded onto ships after crossing overland from the deserts and plains of Asia or ports on the Red Sea and Persian Gulf.

Little is known of the sorts of vessels that composed the Byzantine merchant marine. However, what has been garnered from wrecks suggests that they were similar to their Roman precursors. The largest found was about 200 feet (60 meters) long. The ships usually had a single mast, a large triangular sail, and a wide beam. The goods were often transported in large ceramic vessels, which were the equivalent of contemporary shipping containers.

Some of the port cities developed local industries that modified the trade goods. For instance the port of Tyre, in what is today Lebanon, was famous for dyeing silk and other fabrics using pigments derived from the murex, a spiny mollusk that inhabits the waters of the eastern Mediterranean. The rich purple hue would become the color used for imperial and later ecclesiastical garments in the Eastern and Western Roman Empires. Even today this color holds a prominent place in Christian religious vestments.

Somewhat later it was the imported riches of Byzantium that made the maritime kingdoms of the Italian peninsula wealthy and politically powerful. Other cities on the Italian and European peninsulas also developed local industries derived from the Middle East or farther east. It was not just goods that were being transported, but technologies as well. Many of the traditions of agriculture, metallurgy, and textile arts continue to be successful today. Venice is still known for its fine Murano glass industry, which began as a result of influences from the east before the first millennium.

By the thirteenth century European crusaders grew so envious of the wealth of the Byzantines that they sacked Constantinople during the Fourth Crusade. During the pillaging virtually all of the riches accumulated over a millennium of trade with the East were carried off to Venice and other European capitals. Constantinople would never fully recover. When it fell to the Ottoman Turks in 1452 the age of European exploration had already begun, and the overland Silk Road linking Anatolia with Beijing was only a minor element of transcontinental trade.

A man using murex to dye cloth

CONSTANTINOPLE BECOMES ISTANBUL

In May of 1453—after a vicious two-month siege during which the last Byzantine emperor, Constantine XI, died on the walls defending his beloved city—Constantinople was conquered and taken over by the Ottoman Turks, led by Sultan Mehmed II. Immediately upon seizing control, the Sultan declared it the capital of the Ottoman Empire and changed its name to Istanbul. Constantinople was no more. After it was looted and the Byzantine religious hierarchy was murdered on the high altar, the Hagia Sophia—for many centuries the most magnificent church in Christendom—became the region's greatest mosque, and the city became a center of the Muslim world.

In a convention of medieval warfare, Mehmed allowed the Ottoman army three days to plunder their prize. By no means was his intention to lay waste to the city, but like the Crusaders a couple centuries earlier, their pillaging did destroy much of it.

Understanding the jewel that he had acquired, he set about bringing it back to life. Thus began a period of rebirth and growth, as well as a return to tolerance and multiculturalism. In seeking to rejuvenate the new capital, Mehmed created the Grand Bazaar, one of the largest covered marketplaces in the world, and he encouraged the return of Catholic and Greek Orthodox residents alike, as well as opening the gates to Muslims, Jews, and Christians of all denominations. He also began an ambitious construction program, including the building of numerous monuments, schools, hospitals, public baths, and mosques. Ground was broken for Topkapi Sarayi in 1462, a magnificent palace that would serve as his official residence and go on to house the sultans for some four hundred years.

Constantine XI

Sultan Mahmud II

In the mid-1500s, under the reign of Suleyman the Magnificent (1494–1566), many impressive works of art and architecture, including the Suleymaniye Mosque, were created throughout the Ottoman Empire, and Istanbul once again thrived as a center of politics and commerce. The Ottoman arts of ceramics, calligraphy, and miniatures flourished. The population had grown to nearly one million by the end of the eighteenth century.

Progress and Problems

During the 1800s, under the progressive Sultan Mahmud II (1735–1839) and beyond, Istanbul became more and more westernized. Bridges were constructed spanning the natural harbor known as the Golden Horn, and railroads soon connected the city to the rest of the European network. The introduction of modern technology such as electricity, telephones, and trams followed.

As hard as its leaders tried to keep pace with the other great cities of the world, their efforts at modernization were not enough to keep the Ottoman regime strong as the nineteenth century gave way to the twentieth. A movement known as the Young Turk Revolution brought down Sultan Abdul Hamid II (1842–1918), and a series of wars beset the struggling capital—culminating in World War I, during which Istanbul was occupied by the British, French, and Italian armies.

The last Ottoman sultan, Mehmed VI, was sent into exile in 1922, and the Turkish War of Independence concluded with the end of the occupation, the signing of the Treaty of Lausanne, and the establishment of the Republic of Turkey.

Right: Topkapi Sarayi

Modern Republic

Perhaps surprisingly, Istanbul was passed over as the capital of the new republic in favor of the more centrally located Ankara. Nevertheless, in the 1940s and '50s, substantial investment was made in the infrastructure of Istanbul, yielding new public squares, wide boulevards, and tree-lined avenues.

In the 1970s, Istanbul's population experienced rapid growth, and the city began to spread out and become the major metropolis it remains today. Its many historical areas make it a popular destination for travelers from all over the world, and it was designated the 2010 European Capital of Culture by the European Union.

The Galata Bridge over Golden Horn Strait

Trading by Sea

As early as two thousand years ago China began trading by sea, but it wasn't until the ninth century that it began to rival the Silk Road as a viable trade route. Chinese ships would sail to destinations like Malacca and India. Arab ships made regular voyages from Baghdad to China and back, their holds laden with a variety of valuable goods. With its easy access to the Persian Gulf, Baghdad became the center of Middle Eastern sea trade.

Arab merchants who traveled by sea specialized first in importing Chinese spices and even silk, and then later in ceramics—heavy, breakable cargo that could be carried more efficiently and safely by ship than by jouncing camel caravan. To keep the fragile cups, bowls, and other items from shattering in rough seas, the sailors stacked them in tall stoneware jars.

Still, few Europeans sailed the Indian Ocean until around 1500, when Portuguese explorer Vasco da Gama rounded the southern tip of Africa for the first time. The intrepid traveler Marco Polo was an exception: having journeyed to China along the Silk Road in the late 1200s, he returned west by ship, making several stops along the way.

THE RISE OF SHIPPING

While caravan merchants risked their worldly assets transporting goods over mountains and deserts, other traders placed their bets on the sea. The water route covered some 6,000 miles (9,656 kilometers) from Baghdad to China and took about six months—but this was considerably faster than overland travel, which could take as long as a year. It also afforded merchants destinations beyond the Persian Gulf, primarily to places in the Red Sea. Despite the peril of pirate attacks and treacherous storms, sea trade expanded until eventually it overshadowed the caravan trade in the eleventh century.

A trade ship from an Arabic collection of short stories that originated in the nineth century

Right: Vasco da Gama (1460–1524)

Polos on the Silk Road

Marco Polo (ca. 1254–1324) was neither the first nor the last to travel the Silk Road. Yet for many of us, our first exposure to medieval Asia was through the adapted writings and mythology surrounding his journey. While open to all sorts of interpretation, the story of Marco and the Polo family is both fantastic and familiar. Although it has been part of the Western canon for over seven hundred years, it still has its mysteries and vagaries. It has even been suggested that Polo did not make the voyage at all! Complicating things further is the fact that no complete manuscript exists from the time of Marco Polo. What we are left with is a treatise rife with deletions and a corpus that is an amalgam of different authors writing at different times who often distorted the original story to make the book more salable.

The Polos were a wealthy, aristocratic Venetian family of merchants who traded in goods procured primarily in Byzantium—especially precious gems. It is generally agreed that they journeyed far and wide in search of valuable objects to sell in Italy, becoming rich in the process. The remarkable story of their trip to the Mongol court, however, would not be known except for a peculiar incidence of history that occurred after their monumental journey.

During internecine warfare between the maritime kingdoms of Venice and Genoa at the end of the thirteenth century, Marco Polo was captaining a naval vessel that was taken during battle. He was imprisoned; however, because of his high social standing, he was treated in a "gentlemanly" manner. During his confinement he made the acquaintance of Rustichello da Pisa, a fellow inmate. To bide the time, Marco recounted his travels, which must have sounded like an interplanetary adventure at that time. Taking note, Rustichello began to develop a manuscript of these tales. The project progressed to the point that during his captivity, Marco was allowed to have his notes from his journey brought to the prison to share with Rustichello. The resultant manuscript details one of the great adventures in Western history—a voyage of personal discovery as well as a voyage that illuminated the East to a Western audience. Still read today, the Polo journey remains fresh in its ethnographic detail, sensuality, and its sensitivity to cultures across the Eurasian continent.

A detailed recounting is enough for a book unto itself, so the abbreviated version—as told in two minutes—follows: In about 1260 Marco's father, Niccolo, and his uncle Maffeo made a trading journey to the East. Beginning in Constantinople, they ventured first to the Black Sea where they encountered members of the Golden Horde—Mongols living in the western territory of their empire. Availing themselves of rich trading opportunities, they continued to the city of Bokhara where they came upon an embassy of the Great Khan, Kublai (1215–1294), grandson of Genghis Khan. Under this aegis they traveled onward to the imperial city of Dadu

tinc. Or vous ay compte li comme il auint li yrons auaht et vous
compterons dautres choses.

Marco Polo docks on the straight of Hormuz in The Book of Wonders

(today's Beijing) and met with Kublai himself. Kublai Khan was curious about the larger world, and in 1266 he sent the Polo brothers home to Italy, accompanied by a Mongol ambassador to the pope. He sent a letter with them to the pope that requested one hundred learned people return to China with the Polos to teach the Mongol court about Christianity, Western science, logic, and rhet-

oric. He also asked for specific gifts from the pope, such as oil from the lamp of the Holy Sepulcher in Jerusalem.

The Mongol ambassador abandoned them during the journey, but since they traveled under the Khan's protection, their journey was without incident. In 1271, Pope Gregory X received the letter that the Polos had shepherded.

Soon after, at the request of the Holy See (and to take advantage of obvious trading opportunities), the Polos began a journey back to the court of Kublai with

A cover of Marco Polo's book showing him telling his tales to Rustichello

gifts, the young Marco, and two friars (who later skipped out on the expedition due to fear when they came upon a war zone). On the trip back to Asia the Polos traveled along the classic Silk Road through the oasis towns of Balkh and Kashgar, and finally to Lanzhou and Dadu. On arriving in Dadu they were received by the Khan, who was thrilled with the gifts. The young Marco made a strong impression on the Khan and became a confidant of the master of the largest land empire on the planet.

During the seventeen years that Marco stayed in China he worked as Kublai Khan's emissary in several capacities. He traveled over much of the empire, venturing as far south as Pagan in what is today Myanmar. He imbibed the cultural, culinary, and carnal pleasures of Asia. Marco was a careful observer, and his notes, which have been lost, must have contained a trove of ethnographic detail.

In 1292, the aging Kublai finally let the Polos head homeward. They returned by sea via Singapore and Sumatra to the coast of India, to the Persian Gulf, and then traveled overland to Italy. During the journey, all but sixteen of their party of six hundred perished.

There are many notable things about the Polo/Rustichello manuscript (or manuscripts for that matter, as there are more than 150 different known variants). Obviously the first is that while some locations and historical events are scrupulously documented, others are conspicuously left out. No mention is made of certain geographical details like the Great Wall, cultural phenomena such as foot binding, or culinary practices like the use of chopsticks. To be fair, it should be pointed out that the Great Wall did not achieve its monolithic magnitude until much later during the Ming dynasty (1368–1644), foot binding was not a prevalent practice in the Mongol court, and the use of chopsticks may have seemed just as unusual to the Polos as the use of forks, as modern sorts of tableware did not become popular in Italy until the fourteenth century.

Accurate architectural and geographic details like the presence of the Guangli Bridge (which is now also known as the Marco Polo Bridge because of his acute description) on the outskirts of Beijing, the canals and pleasure palaces of Hangzhou, and the Imperial Palace (the forerunner of the Forbidden City) are described in detail. Inventions such as paper money and the use of coal as a fuel, which was unknown to thirteenth- and fourteenth-century Europeans, were mentioned and

seemed preposterous to Europeans at the time.

Yet, curiously, there is no mention of the Polos in any contemporary Mongol or Chinese texts. This is a fact that has confused scholars for decades and has often been used as evidence that the journey was fiction, or at least highly embellished. One detail remains, however: On their return journey the Polos accompanied the Mongol princess Koekecin, who was destined to be married to a Persian king. Unreported in Western chronicles at the time, this fact was widely recounted in Mongol and Chinese sources and thus points to the potential truth behind the tales told by Marco Polo.

Marco Polo before Kublai Khan

ACROSS THE SEAS

In 851, an Arab traveler told of his sea voyage from the Persian Gulf to the Chinese port city of Guangzhou, formerly known in English as Canton. The map at the beginning of this chapter shows the route, along with the real and imagined wonders described in his own words. Clearly, long-range sea travel was perceived to be an almost mythic undertaking at the time.

Siraf
"The goods are carried to Siraf from Basra, Oman, and other ports, and then they are loaded on the [boats bound for China]."

Indian Ocean
"In this [sea] is found a fish that appears occasionally. It has herbs and shells growing on its back. The captains of boats sometimes lay anchor against it, thinking it to be an island, but when they realize their mistake they set sail from it."

Laccadive and Maldive Islands
"On these islands, ambergris of enormous sizes is thrown up; sometimes each piece is as big as a house or so."

Sri Lanka
"Around this mountain there are mines of precious stone: rubies, topaz, and blue sapphire."

Bay of Bengal
"Sometimes in this sea, one notices a white cloud casting its shadows on the boats; then a long, thin tongue begins to appear from it until this tongue joins the water of the sea. So, because of this, the sea water starts agitating like a hurricane, and when the hurricane overtakes the boat, it swallows it up."

Sumatra
"In this island, elephants are found in large numbers, and it has brazil-wood and bamboos. It also has a tribe who are cannibals."

Paracel Reefs
"These are mountains in the sea. Between each of the two mountains of the sea, there is a passage through which the boats pass."

Guangzhou
"The people of China are handsome and tall. . . . Among all human beings, they have the blackest hair and their womenfolk let their hair float about."

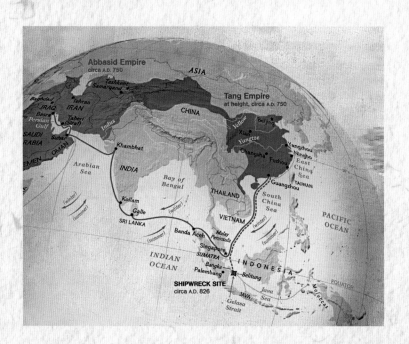

A Tight Ship as Fast as the Wind

Could a boat made without nails be strong enough to withstand the monsoon winds of the Indian Ocean? Believe it or not, yes! For hundreds of years, Middle Eastern merchants sailed on such ships, made of durable teak or coconut wood imported from India or Indonesia. Shipbuilders stitched the planks together with coir, a cord made by twisting fibers of coconut husks. Then they sealed the seams with resin or pitch mixed with whale oil to keep everything durable and watertight.

The most popular boat was the dhow, which was lightweight and maneuverable and sat high on the water. Traditional dhows were rigged with a specially invented sail called a lateen. It was triangular and supported by a diagonal bar attached to the mast that allowed the boat to tack, or sail across the wind.

This illustration shows the stitching method used to sew planks of a ship together and a cross section revealing a cargo hold.

When sailing the Indian Ocean, seamen took advantage of predictable monsoon winds, which blew from the northeast in winter and from the southwest in summer. Arab ships typically sailed down the Persian Gulf in September or October. If they managed to time it just right, they could catch the gentle southwestern monsoon through the South China Sea in April or May.

To track progress when traveling north or south, Arab navigators used a *kamal*, a simple device made up of a knotted string running through a hole in the middle of a small wooden card. Each knot corresponded to the latitude of a well-known port. A sailor held the string in his teeth by the final knot and aligned the bottom of the card with the horizon. Then he slid the card along the string until the top aligned with the pole star. The latitude of the ship could be gauged by the nearest knot.

Left: A ship in a storm
Below: A kamal

SINBAD SAILS AGAIN

Early Arab stories (shared widely in many versions of *One Thousand and One Arabian Nights*, which we learned about earlier) tell of a merchant named Sinbad who sailed the trade routes between Baghdad and China and had extraordinary adventures along the way. In 1980, the British explorer Timothy Severin set out to retrace the voyages of Sinbad in a traditional Arab dhow he named the *Sohar*.

The *Sohar* was built from planks of *aini* wood, which comes from the tropical forests of India. They were sewn together with coconut cord from the Laccadive Islands. Setting sail in late autumn, Severin completed the voyage from Muscat, Oman, to Guangzhou, China, in about seven months—just in time to escape the late summer typhoons.

الساحر بابغ

من المنزل فلغفلة اللصّ ودخل المنزل

السلام الكادي ... القسم الليلة ظهرا ... النهار الازهر ... والمنزل يغ ... دروسب

CERAMICS

The rise of trade between eastern and western Asia inspired ceramic artists to create colorful new wares that could be traded for glass and other goods. In Arab and Persian households, clay pots with colorful glazes, as well as fine white porcelain from Chinese kilns, were especially prized. Over time, potters in both China and the Middle East developed new styles and techniques, as the flow of trade in both directions sparked the interchange of ideas and artistic forms.

A Passion for Porcelain

By the early 600s, during the Tang dynasty, Chinese craftsmen had mastered the technique for making porcelain—a ceramic material with a fine texture that is especially strong. The white clay used to create it is rich in kaolinite (thus, it was named *kaolin*) and other silicate minerals. It is fired at very high temperatures—over 2,460 degrees Fahrenheit (1,350 degrees Celsius)—for a hard, white finish that has many of the qualities of glass. In the early 800s, an Arab traveler watched in awe as Chinese potters made "goblets as thin as flasks, through which the sparkle of water can be seen." These delicate wares were made of porcelain.

For many centuries, potters in the Middle East strove to match the translucent beauty of Chinese porcelain, but kaolin was not available in Islamic lands. Yet, by working with their own materials, Islamic artists made other stunning discoveries, including a wide range of vivid glazes.

Above: A bowl from the Tang dynasty

Left: A bottle from the Sui dynasty

Below: A bowl from the Tang dynasty, with a three-color glaze

Approximating Porcelain

Not all of the pottery produced in China (or elsewhere) was porcelain, of course. In Changsha, a busy Chinese city in what is now Hunan Province, pottery workshops mass-produced goods for the foreign market, just as many Chinese manufacturers do today. Bowls with loose, flowing patterns were made in large batches to meet high demand overseas.

By coating fine clay with white slip—a creamy mixture of clay and water—a Chinese potter could tint an earthenware dish to look something like porcelain, though it was more durable and less precious. In later centuries, more complex patterns of blue-and-white ware would become all the rage in Europe. The blue came from cobalt, a mineral imported from Iran.

Left: A thief slips away with a merchant's vase.

Above: Firing porcelain vases during the Ming dynasty

During the Abbasid era (750–1258), potters in the Middle East developed their own techniques for creating the look of Chinese porcelain. One popular method was to coat the clay with an opaque white glaze. The makers often decorated their work by inscribing them with passages from the Qu'ran in cobalt-blue Kufic calligraphy.

In the 1100s, Islamic craftsmen developed a fine-textured clay by mixing crushed quartz with small amounts of ground-up glaze and natural white clay. The resulting pottery, known as fritware, was snow-white like porcelain. Potters decorated it with brightly colored glazes.

Right: A thirteenth century fritware bowl painted with cobalt

Below: An earthenware bowl from the Abbasid era with a Kufic inscription

EXCHANGE OF ARTISTRY

From East to West

The graceful shape of the blue and white bowls shown here traveled from China to the Middle East, thanks to the maritime trade. The Chinese dish is white-glazed porcelain, while the other is fritware with a tin-enamel glaze, a specialty of Iran developed in an attempt to replicate porcelain.

From West to East

Chinese artists making porcelain vases borrowed a shape from imported Islamic glassware. Markets of the Middle East did a brisk business selling Chinese ceramics colored with the pale green glaze known as celadon.

Islamic Ingenuity

The creation of Islamic ceramics reached its peak as potters learned to paint a second layer of glaze over the first to make detailed, multicolored designs. This bowl illustrates a story from the Persian *Book of Kings*, in which a hero is challenged by his servant to prove his skill in archery.

As important as the Silk Road was for the exchange of ideas, stories, discoveries, and traditions, the sea trade provided just as critical a conduit for cultural cross-pollination.

THE JOURNEY'S END

Your journey through history to the ancient cities of the Silk Road is complete. But these cities—Xi'an, Turfan, Samarkand, Baghdad, and Istanbul—still exist today. In some ways, they have changed dramatically. In others, they remain the same. Xi'an remains a bustling metropolis, Turfan is an oasis of orchards and vineyards in the desert, Samarkand's beauty has endured the ages, Baghdad continues on as a centerpiece of the Islamic world, and Istanbul's ports still thrive. Their history is as expansive as the Silk Road itself, and their stories continue to be written and discovered to this day.

Previous page: This fifteenth-century painting is attributed to a Turkish artist but shows Chinese influence and pottery.

Right: This modern-day caravan is traveling in much the same way Silk Road patrons have been for centuries.

Further Reading

Shadow of the Silk Road, Colin Thubron, Great Britain: Chatto & Windus 2006 (New York: HarperCollins Publishers 2007).

The Silk Road Journey with Xuanzang (Revised and Updated), Sally Hovey Wriggins, Boulder, Colo: Westview Press, 2004.

Genghis Khan and the Mongol Empire, Jean-Paul Roux, France: Gallimard 2002 (trans. New York: Abrams 2003).

Marco Polo: From Venice to Xanadu, Laurence Bergreen, New York: Knopf, 2007.

The Silk Road, Sven Hedin, Great Britain: Macmillan and Co. Ltd, 1938 (Great Britain: Tauris Parke Paperbacks, 2009).

Life Along the Silk Road, Susan Whitfield, Berkeley, CA: University of California Press, 1999.

Silk Road: Monks, Warriors & Merchants, Luce Boulnois; translated by Helen Loveday, Hong Kong: Odyssey Books & Guides 2008.

The Silk Road Gourmet, Laura Kelley, Bloomington, IN: 2009.

Picture Credits

age fotostock
p. 43 © The British Library
pp. 60, 104–105 © Shigeki Tanaka
p. 74 © Andrea Pistolesi
pp. 100–101, 118 © Panorama Media
p. 115 © Morales
pp. 138–139 © Angela Prati
p. 186–187 © Targa

akg-images
pp. 150 (Step 1), 181 right: © Gerard Degeorge
p. 194 top: © Philippe Maillard

Alamy
pp. 44, 102 bottom, 150 far left, 150 (Step 2), 151 (Steps 3–5):
    © INTERFOTO
pp. 134–135, 141: © dbimages
p. 137: North Wind Picture Archives
pp. 222–223: © MARKA
p. 224: © Art Gallery Collection

© American Museum of Natural History
pp. 65, 85: photos by Denis Finnin
p. 90: Roy Chapman Andrews
pp. 111, 112, 114 (spices), 116, 117, 119, 120, 198, 250, 258: photos by
    Rod Mickens

Art Archive
p. 18: photo © Hsien-Min Yang/NGS Image Collection
p. 37: photo © Dagli Orti
p. 57: photo © The British Library Board
p. 87: photo © Dagli Orti/Musée Guimet, Paris
p. 136: photo © Alfredo Dagli Orti/Musée Archéologique, Naples
p. 180 right: photo © Gianni Dagli Orti/National Library, Cairo
pp. 183, 215: photos © Dagli Orti/University Library, Istanbul
p. 184: photo © Kharbine-Tapabor
p. 193: Bodleian Library, University of Oxford
p. 220: © Dagli Orti/Historika Muséet, Stockholm
pp. 242–243: photo © Dagli Orti/Topkapi Palace Museum

Art Resource
p. 19: photo © Scala
pp. 39, 79 middle, 193 bottom: photos © Werner Forman
p. 78: Image © The Metropolitan Museum of Art. Textile with Floral Medal-
    lion, Late 8th–early 9th century. China, Tang dynasty (618–907). Woven
    silk: weft-faced compound twill. Overall: 24 x 28 in. (61 x 71.1 cm).
    Purchase, Joseph Pulitzer Bequest, 1996 (1996.103.1).
p. 82: Image © The Metropolitan Museum of Art. Interior of a Portable
    Shrine. 5th–6th century. Pakistan (ancient Gandhara). Phyllitic schist,
    H. 3 7/16 in. (8.7 cm). Samuel Eilenberg Collection, Gift of Samuel
    Eilenberg, 1987 (1987.142.53).
p. 83 top: Image © The Metropolitan Museum of Art. Interior of a Por-
    table Shrine. 5th–6th century. Phyllitic schist. H. 3 7/16 in. (8.7 cm).
    Back. Samuel Eilenberg Collection, Gift of Samuel Eilenberg, 1987
    (1987.142.53).
pp. 84, 231: photos © Snark
p. 103: Image © The Metropolitan Museum of Art. Jun, Liu (fl. Ca. 1475–ca.
    1505). Remonstrating with the Emperor; Najian. Hanging scroll; ink
    and color on silk. Image: 65 1/2 x 41 3/4 inc. (166.4 x 106 cm) Overall
    with mounting: 116 x 50 in. (294.6 x 127 cm) Overall with knobs: 116 x
    54 in. (294.6 x 137.2 cm). Ex coll.: C.C. Wang Family, Gift of the Oscar
    L. Tang Family, 2005 (2005.494.3).
pp. 109, 185, 239 bottom: Bildarchiv Preussischer Kulturbesitz
p. 122: Image © The Metropolitan Museum of Art. Glass oinochoe (jug), late
    1st century BCE–early 1st century CE. Roman, Early Imperial, Augustan
    or Julio-Claudian. Glass, H. 7 1/8 in. (18.1 cm); diameter 3 3/8 in. (8.6
    cm). Gift of J. Pierpont Morgan, 1917 (17.194.170).
pp. 149, 159 top: Digital Images © 2009 Museum Associates/LACMA
p. 152: Image © The Metropolitan Museum of Art. Engraver: Lei Yanmei,
    Chinese, 9th–10th century. The Greatly Merciful, Greatly Compassionate
    Rescuer from Suffering, the Bodhisattva Avalokitesvara. China, dated
    947. Woodblock print; ink and color on paper. Image 18 3/4 x 12 3/4 in.
    (47.6 x 32.4 cm) Mat size 29 1/2 x 23 in. (74.9 x 58.4 cm). Gift of Paul
    Pelliot through the Morgan Library, 1924 (CP5).
p. 155: Image © The Metropolitan Museum of Art. Qur'an manuscript from
    North Africa. Ca. 1250-1300. Ink, colors, and gold on vellum, Page: 10
    1/4 x 8 9/16 in. (26 x 21.7 cm) Mat: 19 1/4 x 14 1/4 in. (48.9 x 36.2 cm).
    Rogers Fund, 1937 (37.21).
p. 158: Image © The Metropolitan Museum of Art. Leaf from an Arabic

translation of the *Materia Medica of Dioscorides* ("Preparation of Medicine from Honey"), dated 1224. Iraq, Baghdad School. Colors and gold on paper; 12.5 x 8.5 in. (31.8 x 21.6 cm). Rogers Fund, 1913 (13.152.6)

p. 159 bottom: The Pierpont Morgan Library. Gospel Book. MS M.640, fol. 100v. Photo: David A. Loggie.

p. 166: © Harvard Art Museum. Two Standing, Braying Camels, One Buff, One White, Their Backs Laden with Goods, from the tomb sculpture set. China, 550–577 CE. Molded, medium gray earthenware with cold-painted pigments; localized areas with cold-painted pigments over white ground, 33.5 x 25 x 19.5 cm (13 3/16 x 9 13/16 x 7 11/16 in.). Partial and Promised Gift of Anthony M. Solomon, 2003.193.2. Photo: Imaging Department.

p. 193 bottom: photo © Werner Forman/Topkapi Palace Museum/Art Resource

p. 194: Image © The Metropolitan Museum of Art. Bottle. Attributed to Egypt or Syria, 7th–early 8th century. Glass; free-blown, tooled with applied decoration, H. 7 15/16 in. (20.14 cm), Diam. 3 7/32 in. (8.24 cm). Museum Accession (x.21.210)

p. 200 top: Image © The Metropolitan Museum of Art. Glass Goblet. Islamic, 8th–9th CE. Attributed to Iraq or Syria. Inscribed in Arabic: 'Blessings from Allah to the owner of the goblet. Drink!' Transparent pale greenish-blue glass; free-blown, tooled and incised glass, H. 4 5/8 in. (11.7 cm) Diam. Of rim: 3 9/16 in. (9 cm). Purchase, Joseph Pulitzer Bequest, 1965 (65.173.1).

p. 218: photo © Erich Lessing

p. 239 middle: Image © The Metropolitan Museum of Art. Bottle. China, probably Sui dynasty (581–618). Stoneware with incised and impressed decoration under glaze (Northern ware), 10 x 4 7/8 in. (25.4 x 12.4 cm). Gift of Ernest Erickson Foundation, 1985 (1985.214.130).

p. 240 left: photo © SEF

© Asian Art Museum of San Francisco
p. 81: The Avery Brundage Collection, B60P521. Used by permission.
p. 202: The Avery Brundage Collection, B60P1856. Used by permission.

Asia Society, New York
p. 80 top: Mr. and Mrs. John D. Rockefeller 3rd Collection, 1979.117
p. 91: Mr. and Mrs. John D. Rockefeller 3rd Collection, 1979.113

Aurora Photos
p. 221: © Carl Wolinsky

Bibliothèque Nationale de France
pp. 147, 154, 182, 192 left, 228, 236 left, 238, 246

Bodleian Library, University of Oxford
p. 188: MS. Huntington 214, folio 1 recto

The Bridgeman Art Library
pp. 181 (left), 189

© The British Library Board
p. 20: Photo 392/26 (250)
p. 148: Or. 8212/921
p. 156: Or. 8212/499, recto
p. 157: Or. 8210/P.2, frontispiece and text
p. 180 left: Or. 2784, f.96
p. 201: Or. 6573, ff.210v-211
pp. 202–203: OIOC Photo 392/26 (588)

Brooklyn Museum
p. 240 top right: *Blue and White Bowl with Kufic Inscription*, Abbasid, 9th century Ceramic; earthenware, painted in cobalt blue on an opaque white glaze. H. 1 5/16 Diam. 5 3/16 in. Brooklyn Museum 74.195 Gift of Ernest Erickson

p. 240 bottom right: *Blue and White Bowl with Radial Design.* 13th century Ceramic; fritware, painted in cobalt blue under a transparent glaze, H. 3 11/16 in. Diameter at mouth: 6 15/16 in. Thickness of rim: 9/16 in. Diameter at foot: 3 5/16 in. Brooklyn Museum 75.2 Gift of Mr. and Mrs. Thomas S. Brush

p. 241 right: *Bowl Depicting Bahram Gur and Azada*, Seljuq, late 12th–early 13th century Ceramic, mina'i or haft rangi ware; fritware, covered with a white glaze, then polychrome under- and overglaze painted, H. 4 Diam. 8 5/16 in. Brooklyn Museum 86.227.11 Gift of the Ernest Erickson Foundation, Inc.

Cleveland Art Museum
pp. 66, 67–68, 69–70, 71, 72: Attributed to Lian Kai (Chinese). *Sericulture (The Process of Making Silk)*, details, early 13th Century. Handscroll; ink and color on silk, first section 26.5 x 92.2 cm; second section 27.5 x 92.2 cm; third section 27.3 x 93.5 cm. © The Cleveland Museum of Art. John L. Severance Collection 1977.5

p. 170 top: *Textile with Boar's Head.* Iran or Central Asia, Sogdiana, late 6th–early 8th century, late 500s–early 700s, Tapestry weave; wool and linen, 20.7 x 25.15 cm. © The Cleveland Museum of Art. John L. Severance Fund 1950.509

Columbia University
p. 190: Smith Oriental Manuscripts
pp. 191, 192 right

Corbis
pp. 107, 178-179, 210-211, 233
pp. 16–17: © Keren Su
p. 21: © Wang Miao/Redlink

p. 22: © Mimmo Jodice
pp. 28–29: © Science Faction
pp. 31, 124–125: © George Steinmetz
pp. 34–35: © Mu Xiang Bin/Redlink
p. 36: © Luca Tettoni
p. 38: © The Gallery Collection
pp. 46–47: © Antonia Tozer/Jon Arnold Images
p. 63 top: © Carl & Ann Purcell
p. 63 bottom: © Ryan Pyle
p. 75: © Thomas Hartwell
pp. 92–93: © Tibor Bognar
p. 121: © Liang Zhuoming
pp. 126–127: © Zhang Hongxiang/Xinhua Press
p. 167: © Michel Setboun/Sygma
pp.170–171: © Manca Juvan
p. 225: © Yann Arthus-Bertrand
p. 229: © Stapleton Collection
p. 219: © Historical Picture Archive

eStock Travel
pp. 54–55: © HP Huber/SIME

Fotolia
p. 102 top: © Valeriy Shanin
p. 214: © Angelo Giampiccolo

Getty Images
p. 23: © Imagno
pp. 26–27: SSPL
p. 40: © Gallo Images
pp. 58–59, 106: © Keren Su/China Span
p. 79 right: The Bridgeman Art Library
p. 140: © C. Sappa/DeAgostini
pp. 160–161: © James Morris/The Image Bank
p.232: Hulton Archive

Hemis.fr
pp. 226–227: © BODY Philippe

© Hu Chui
pp. 108, 123 (both)

iStockphoto.com
p. 114 (dates): © ac_bnphotos
p.163: © Eric Isselée
p. 199 bottom: © Muha04

p. 221 top: © Pavle Marjanovic

Library of Congress
pp. 24–25, 110, 113, 144–145

Library of Congress, Geography and Map Division
pp. 6–14, 49–52, 95–98, 129–132, 173–176, 205–208, 251

© The Mariner's Museum, Newport News, VA
p. 236 right

Mary Evans Picture Library
p. 165

The Minneapolis Institute of Arts
p. 239 top: Chinese, Tang Dynasty. *Bowl.* Gift of funds from William G. Seidenberg and Cliff and Sue Roberts. Minneapolis Institute of Arts accession number: 93.8

Museum of Fine Arts, Boston
p. 73: Attributed to: Emperor Huizong, Chinese, 1082–1135. *Court ladies preparing newly woven silk,* detail. Chinese, Northern Song Dynasty, early 12th century. Ink, color, and gold on silk. 37 x 145.3 cm (14 9/16 x 57 3/16 in.) Special Chinese and Japanese Fund, 12.886

National Geographic Stock
pp. 234, 235: Fernando G. Baptista

The Nelson-Atkins Museum of Art, Kansas City, Missouri
p. 83 bottom: *Traveling Shrine of Vairocana and Eight Bodhisattvas on a Garbhadhatu Mandala,* Chinese, 9th–10th century C.E., Tang Dynasty (618–906 C.E.). Sandalwood with traces of red and green coloring, 12 1/4 x 14 inches (31.1 x 35.6 cm). Purchase: William Rockhill Nelson Trust, 44-18. Photograph: Robert Newcombe

Philadelphia Museum of Art
p. 241 left: Accession # 1944-20-166A. *Dish.* Artist/maker unknown. Chinese, Tang Dynasty (618-907). Glazed porcelain (Xing or Ding ware), 618–907. 1 3/8 x 6 1/4 inches (3.5 x 15.8 cm) Gift of Major General and Mrs. William Crozier, 1944
p. 241 middle: Accession #1919-357. *Dish.* Artist/maker unknown. Iranian, Persian, Seljuk Period (1038–1220). Glazed ceramic, c. 1150. 1 1/2 x 6 1/8 inches (3.8 x 15.6 cm) Purchased with Special Museum Funds, 1919

Photolibrary
pp. 30, 89, 124: © Tao Images

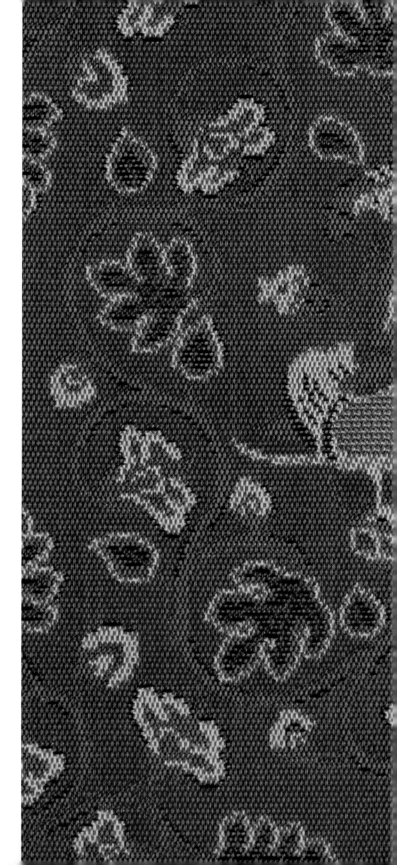

About the Map

Below is the original version of the map used on pages 6–14, 49–52, 95–98, 129–132, 173–176, and 205–208. It is from the Library of Congress, Geography and Map Division. It is by the French cartographer Guillaume de L'Isle and was first published in 1700.

The Silk Road era was a time when the boundaries of countries and cultures blurred and shifted frequently; a time when travelers were not always sure what they would find beyond the next mountain pass or sand dune. This map was chosen because of its aesthetic and its representation of a time when the lines on a map were more yielding than they are today.

The place names have been rewritten to reflect the cities and landforms relevant to the Silk Road. The topography and boundary lines have not been altered from the original with the exception of the mountains surrounding the Taklimakan desert, which were redrawn to more accurately reflect this region so crucial to the story of the Silk Road.

Index

Stein, Aurel (1862–1943), 31, 43–44
stele, Nestorian, 85, *85*
steppes, trade routes from, 199
"The Stonecutter Who Was Never Satisfied" (tale), 146
storax bark, 117, *117*
stupas
    at Sanchi, India, *36*
    in Xinjiang Province, China, *46–47*
Sucandra, 82
Sulemaniye Mosque, 224
Suleyman the Magnificent (1494–1566), 224, *224*
Sumatra, 234
Syrian Desert, 31
Sythian metalworking, 199

т

Taklimakan Desert, 31–32
    Buddhist grottoes in, 35
    Kuga Canyon in, *31*
    road through, *92–93*
    sand dunes, *16–17*
Taklimakan region
    Chinese conquest of, 40
    tourism in, 46
tales
    by Scheherazade. *see One Thousand and One Arabian Nights*
    from the Silk Road, 146–147
Talipot palm leaf documents, 149, *149*
Tamerlane (Timur the Lame, 1336–1405), 136, *138–139,* 139, 185
Tang dynasty (618–907 CE)
    papermaking in, 156
    porcelain ceramics in, 239, *239*
    tea drinking in, 199
    trade during, 16

Turfan during, 100
Xi'an during, 36, 54
Taoism (Daoism), 84–85
Taxila, 28
"Tea and Horse Caravan Road," 198–199
tea drinking, 198–199
Tejaprabba Buddha, *88*
temperature, along Silk Road, 28
terracotta army, 54, 62–63, *62–63*
Theodosius I, 213
Thermal spring, Xi'an, *54–55*
Timur the Lame (Tamerlane, 1336–1405), 136, *138–139,* 139, 185
Timurid dynasty, 136
tomb figures
    camels, *166*
    made from paper, 108, *108*
    from tomb of Qin Shi Huang, 54, 62–63, *62–63*
    from tomb of Zhang Xiong, 108, *108*
Topkapi Sarayi, Istanbul, 222, *225*
tourism, in Taklimakan region, 46
trade
    land *vs.* sea, 37, 39, 228, 234, *234. see also* maritime trade
    under Mongol rule, 39
    during Tang dynasty, 16
    through Europe and Mediterranean, 220
trade goods, 79–81, *79–81.* see also individual types of goods, e,g. ceramics
    carriage by sea, 37, 39, 228
travel time, 28
Travels with Marco Polo (Polo), 39
"tribute missions," to Chinese emperors, 102, *103*

Turfan, 27, 32
    climate and geography of, 105
    contemporary, 105
    Gaochang temple complex near, 44
    in Han dynasty, 100
    historic rulers of, 100
    history of, 100, 102, 105
    markets of, *110,* 111–121, *113*
    mummies discovered at, 107
    population of, 105
    rainfall amounts in, 105
    Russian interest in, 40
    in Tang dynasty, 100
Turfan region
    desertification in, 22
    settlements in Han dynasty, 21
    Turkic Uyghurs in, 102
    Uyghurs in, 108–109
Turkish War of Independence, 224
Tyre, Lebanon, 221

u

Ulugh Beg observatory, 140, *142–143*
Umayyad dynasty (661–750), papermaking and, 158, 159
Uyghurs
    art of, *102*
    princesses, fresco depicting, *44*
    in Turfan region, 108–109
    Turkic, 102
Uzbekistan, *caravanserai* in, *24–25*

v

vegetables, transporting, *112*

vellum documents, 149
    Qur'an, 149, 155, *155*
Venice, Italy, 221, *221*
Viking funerary pits, Buddha images in, 220
vineyards, around Turfan, 105, *115*

w

Wang Jie, 157
Wang Yuanlu (ca. 1849–1931), 43
Warner, Langdon (1881–1955), *45*
Warring Sates period (475–221 BCE), 19, 54
water
    failure in supply. *see* desertification
    for irrigation (*karez* water systems), 28, 105, 124, *124–125,* 126
    rainfall amounts, 28
    thermal spring at Xi'an, *54–55*
water clock, 192
water conservation, in camels, 164–166
wax tablets, 149
wells (*karez* water systems), 28, 105, 124, *124–125,* 126
"Western Peace." *see* Xi'an
wine, 114, 200
wine peddler (figurine), 81, *81*
wood tablets, 149
wood-block printing, 152, *152,* 157
    Buddhism and, 157–158
wool, 120, *120*
writing
    art of, Arabic alphabet and, 200–202
    calligraphy, 200. *see also* Kufic calligraphy

About the Contributors

Mark A. Norell, Curator and Chair, Division of Paleontology

For the last two decades, Mark Norell has been one of the team leaders of the joint American Museum of Natural History/Mongolian Academy of Sciences expeditions to the Gobi Desert of Mongolia. With the discovery of extraordinarily well-preserved fossils in Mongolia, Dr. Norell and the team have generated new ideas about bird origins and the groups of dinosaurs to which modern birds are most closely related. Dr. Norell, who came to the American Museum of Natural History in 1989, was one of the Gobi Desert Expedition team members who discovered Ukhaa Tolgod in 1993, the world's richest vertebrate fossil site dating from the Cretaceous. Among the discoveries are the first embryo of a meat-eating dinosaur, the primitive avialian *Mononykus*, and an *Oviraptor* found nesting on a brood of eggs, the first evidence of parental care among dinosaurs. In addition to fieldwork in the Gobi, Patagonia, the Chilean Andes, and the Sahara, Dr. Norell was part of the team that in 1998 announced the discovery in northeastern China of two 120-million-year-old dinosaur species, both of which show unequivocal evidence of true feathers. Currently, he continues work on the evolutionary relationships of dinosaurs and modern birds, has named new dinosaurs like *Alioramus* and *Byronosaurus*, and has developed new ways of looking at fossils using CT scans and imaging.

Dr. Norell has also curated Museum exhibitions *Dinosaurs: Ancient Fossils, New Discoveries* (May 2005) and *Mythic Creatures: Dragons, Unicorns and Mermaids* (May 2007, with Laurel Kendall and Richard Ellis). Recent books include *Discovering Dinosaurs* (1995), *A Nest of Dinosaurs* (2000), *Unearthing the Dragon* (2005), and the coffee-table book *The Dinosaur Hunters: The Extraordinary Story of the Men and Women Who Discovered Prehistoric Life,* published with co-author Lowell Dingus in 2008. Dr. Norell came to the American Museum of Natural History in 1989 from Yale University, where he was a lecturer in the Department of Biology. In 1988 he earned his Ph.D. in biology from Yale, where, since 1991, he has been Adjunct Assistant Professor of biology.

Denise Patry Leidy, Curator, Department of Asian Art, The Metropolitan Museum of Art

Denise Leidy received both her Masters degree and Ph.D. from Columbia University. Dr. Leidy has traveled widely on the Silk Road, both as an independent scholar and as member of multinational academic study groups. She is a specialist in Chinese sculpture and decorative arts, and has published widely on these topics, as well as working on numerous exhibitions including the 2004 *China: Dawn of a Golden Age 200–750 A.D.*, and the 2010 *The World of Khubilai: Chinese Art in the Yuan Dynasty*, both of which were presented in The Metropolitan Museum of Art. Her recent publications include *Wisdom Embodied: Chinese Buddhist and Daoist Sculpture in the Metropolitan Museum of Art* (2010), and *The Art of Buddhism: an Introduction to Its History and Meaning* (2008).

Laura Ross

Laura Ross is a writer, editor, and literary agent who lives in New York City. Her career in book publishing has included executive positions at Penguin Books and Simon & Schuster and most recently, she was the Editorial Director of Black Dog & Leventhal Publishers. For Sterling, she has edited new editions of *Walden*, *Leaves of Grass*, *The Sayings of Confucius*, *Common Sense and the Rights of Man*, and *I Ching*, as well as a new collection of the works of Theodore Roosevelt, coming in Spring 2012.

Acknowledgements

Traveling the Silk Road: Ancient Pathway to the Modern World would not have been possible without the support of the staff and trustees of the American Museum of Natural History. This book was produced in conjunction with the nearly eponymous exhibition, created by the American Museum of Natural History under the direction of David Harvey, Sr. Vice President for Exhibition. Portions of this book are drawn from the exhibition text, written by Margaret Dornfeld and John Whitney. William Honeychurch of Yale University provided expert information, especially concerning the Mongol influence on Eurasian trade.

From Sterling Publishing, Katherine Furman and Pamela Horn, in conjunction with the Business Development team at the AMNH brought this book to fruition.

This project was developed with the help and inspiration of people around the globe including those along the Silk Road who have graciously opened their doors to us during our travels. Even today, the influence of this ancient trade route continues to reverberate across the fabric of Eurasian culture and beyond.